SHOTOKAN
TRANSCENDENCE

松濤館を超えて

SHOTOKAN TRANSCENDENCE

松濤館を超えて

BEYOND THE STEALTH AND RIDDLES
OF FUNAKOSHI KARATE

KOUSAKU YOKOTA

横田耕作

To order additional copies of this book, contact:
Azami Press
1-765-242-7988
www.AzamiPress.com
Info@AzamiPress.com

AZAMI PRESS

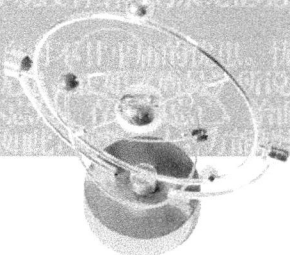

超越篇

DEDICATION
奉納

I dedicate this book to Master Gichin Funakoshi (1868–1957), the founder of Shotokan and the Father of modern karate. I thank him for bringing karate to mainland Japan. Due to his generous contribution and the dedication of his life to *karatedo*, we can enjoy practicing Shotokan all around the world today.

KOUSAKU YOKOTA BIOGRAPHY
経歴

Shihan Kousaku Yokota, eighth *dan*, is a professional *karateka* with extensive experience in various martial arts. With over fifty years of training in Shotokan karate, he specializes in Asai Ryu Bujutsu karate. His wide range of experience includes training in *kobudo* (*nanasetsukon* and nunchaku), in the art of ki, and in the breathing method by Nishino Ryu Kikojutsu. He was a member of the JKA for forty years and then joined the JKS for seven years. In 2013, he founded his organization, ASAI (Asai Shotokan Association International [www.asaikarate.com]) to honor Master Tetsuhiko Asai. Shihan Yokota travels extensively around the world to share the knowledge and techniques of Asai Ryu karate. He is also the partner of Karate Coaching (www.karatecoaching.com), where he extends his karate teaching through Internet media.

ACKNOWLEDGMENTS
感謝の言葉

I dedicate this book, *Shotokan Transcendence*, to Master Funakoshi with a great appreciation for his having brought karate to mainland Japan. Without his selfless effort, we may not have had a Shotokan style of karate today, which we love so much. The last precept of Funakoshi's *Niju Kun* is "Always think deeply and be creative." I am still far from mastering karate, but I try to think deeply and be creative not only in karate but also in everything in my life.

A word of appreciation must be extended to Phillip Kim for his exceptional talent in having created the beautiful cover of this book as he also did with the last two books. I also need to thank Dr. Michael Johnson and Sensei LeRoy O'Neill for their kind assistance in doing the tedious proofreading of my English writing.

I also need to mention that this book almost did not materialize. I encountered a problem with the original publisher, who objected to the way I wrote this book. I am very happy to have found a new partner, Azami Press, and I look forward to working with this company not only for this book but for all the future books I plan to write. I want to thank Mr. Scott Kays, who is the owner of Azami Press and also the sensei of Azamikan Dojo (Shorin Ryu karate).

And, last but not least, to all my sensei, past and present, a sincere thanks for giving me the understanding and knowledge of this great karate style, Shotokan.

Many more people helped me make the creation of this third book possible. From the bottom of my heart, I want to say:

"Thank you very much to all of you."

心より御礼申し上げます。

FOREWORD

By Patrick McCarthy

Hanshi Ninth Dan

Director, International Ryukyu Karate Research Society

Brisbane, Australia

It has been four years since I congratulated the author, Yokota Shihan, for his first book, *Shotokan Myths*, which yielded wonderful success, impressing karate enthusiasts around the world.

To my great pleasure Yokota Shihan continued his quest of embracing the essence of *bunburyodo* [文武両道]. What lies before you, *Shotokan Transcendence*, is the third episode in the author's ongoing work, which goes beyond the myths and enlightenment of mysteries.

Yokota Shihan provides straightforward answers often glossed over or unaddressed. The reader will find the thought-provoking material covered in his work simple and straightforward enough for beginners and yet diverse and comprehensive enough for the well experienced, too. I am confident the way the information is presented is sure to provoke all martial artists to rethink what they already know while challenging them to continue exploring their understandings in order to arrive at a definitive knowledge.

By sharing his thoughts and opinions in this work, Yokota Shihan builds an important bridge linking the past to the present, providing a simple way to accurately understand and pass on the history, technique and philosophy of Shotokan karate to the next generation of learners. His work demonstrates his knowledge of and respect to the legacy of the art while honoring the heritage of those pioneers responsible for developing Shotokan karate.

In *Shotokan Transcendence*, Yokota Shihan unites the courage to speak with unprecedented depth about karate and the talent required for this daring task and shares with us the admirable result. In my opinion, this work is destined to become a modern classic and an important part of the history of Shotokan karate.

FOREWORD

By Samir Berardo

Goju Ryu & Shotokan Practitioner

President, ASAI Brazil

Belem, Brazil

O livro que repousa diante de você possui história. Trata-se do terceiro episódio de uma série notável escrita pelo Shihan Kousaku Yokota. Nos dois primeiros títulos, ao esclarecer mitos e equívocos amplamente aceitos nas escolas de Shotokan de todo o mundo, o autor realizou um feito sem precedentes na literatura sobre o estilo -- e, em grande parte, na do Karate como um todo.

Shotokan Transcendence, como o nome indica, vai além da derrubada dos mitos e esclarecimento dos mistérios, e oferece reflexões de um Shotokan que, já plenamente consciente de si próprio, pode abordar os pormenores da arte com maturidade e profundidade, para muito além do que faria um mero manual de conhecimentos básicos sobre Karate. E contudo essa riqueza de informação é transmitida de forma acessível a todos, com a experiência de um instrutor que consegue ensinar uma mesma lição a todos os alunos do dojo, independentemente do nível de graduação.

Em *Shotokan Transcendence*, Shihan Kousaku Yokota alia a coragem de falar com profundidade inédita sobre o Karate ao talento necessário para essa tarefa ousada, e compartilha conosco o admirável resultado. É um livro que possui história, e que fará parte da história do Karate Shotokan.

English

The book that lies before you has history. This is the third episode of a notable series written by Shihan Kousaku Yokota. In the first two titles, by clarifying myths and misconceptions widely accepted in schools of Shotokan all around the world, the author conducted an unprecedented feat in the literature of the style and largely in that of karate as a whole.

Shotokan Transcendence, as the name implies, goes beyond the overthrow of the myths and enlightenment of mysteries and offers reflections from a Shotokan which, now fully aware of itself, may address the details of the art with maturity and depth, far beyond what a mere karate manual with basic knowledge would do. Yet this wealth of information is conveyed in an accessible manner to all with the experience of an instructor who can teach the same lesson to all students in the dojo, regardless of grade level.

In *Shotokan Transcendence*, Shihan Kousaku Yokota unites the courage to speak with unprecedented depth about karate and the talent required for this daring task and shares with us the admirable result. It is a book that has history and that will be part of the history of Shotokan karate.

FOREWORD

By Roberto Eisenmann III

Shotokan Practitioner

President, ASAI Panama

Panama City, Panama

De la palabra *trascendencia*, se desprenden elementos valiosísimos. Entre ellos, tenemos que la relevancia de un verdadero maestro, más que en su conocimiento, está en transmitirlo y compartirlo. Una vez más, gracias a Shihan Kousaku Yokota, tenemos esa dicha y bendición. Esta tercera entrega nos obsequia un paso más hacia el adentramiento amplio y profundo en la esencia del Shotokan.

Aun cuando para Shihan Yokota ésta constituye su tercera y última entrega, confío que, aprovechando su estado de juventud y salud, haga honor a su encomiable vocación al karate y continúe su docencia, a través de la cual inspira a otros a emprender y seguir la maravillosa senda marcial del *karatedo*.

English

From the meaning of the word *transcendence*, valuable elements emerge. Amongst them, we have that the relevance of a true master, more than in his knowledge, is in his ability to transmit it and share it. Once again, thanks to Shihan Kousaku Yokota, we have that privilege and blessing. This third installment takes us one step closer to the broad and deep essence of Shotokan.

While for Shihan Yokota, this constitutes his third and last installment, I stand confident that, taking advantage of his state of youth and health, he will honor his commendable vocation to karate and continue his teaching, through which he inspires others to undertake and follow the wonderful martial path of *karatedo*.

Foreword

By Stephan Yamamoto

Sixth Dan, Shotokanryu Shushukan

Founding Member, ASAI

St. Leon-Rot, Germany

Nach zweien, für die Shotokan-Welt wichtigen Büchern legt Kosaku Yokota jetzt sein drittes Werk *Shotokan Transcendence* vor und wird damit dem Karate der Gegenwart gerecht.

Karate hat als Kampfkunst, Sportart und Politikum die Welt umrundet und dabei neue Formen inspiriert. Es muss daher als Fundament für das weiterbestehende Interesse und die heutige Vielfalt an Kampfkunst angesehen werden. Aber es muss sich auch von mehreren Seiten Kritik gefallen lassen. Nicht immer finden die neuen Formen Anklang. Und der Diskurs um seine historische wie pragmatische Authentizität droht durch institutionelle Grabenkämpfe zum Stillstand zu kommen.

Heute gibt Karate vielen Menschen Halt und Bestätigung, Möglichkeiten zur sportlichen Betätigung wie auch das Zwischenmenschliche zu pflegen. Dabei sind im Zuge von transkulturellen Flüssen viele Zuschreibungen entstanden, denen nur schwer beizukommen ist. Mit seinen beiden ersten Werken hat Yokota einen wichtigen und erfolgreichen Versuch unternommen, mit alten Mythen aufzuräumen. Er stellte Fragen, die innerhalb der Karate-Welt – und vor allem innerhalb des Shotokan-Diskurses – bis heute nicht populär sind.

Shotokan Transcendence geht den nächsten, logischen Schritt und verweist ganz wörtlich auf das, was nicht gleich offensichtlich ist. Es greift Fragen auf, denen sich gerade die Anhänger des traditionellen Karate heute stellen müssen. Yokotas Antworten schließen die Lücken, die durch die Art und Weise der Lehre – gerade außerhalb Japans – entstanden sind. Das Karate der früheren JKA-Größen Masatoshi Nakayama oder Tetsuhiko Asai dürfte daher für den einen oder anderen vor einem neuen Hintergrund erscheinen. Gerade Asai hat uns wie kein anderer zum Überschreiten der institutionellen Grenzen des

Shotokan-Karate aufgefordert. Yokota Kosaku ist dieser Aufforderung mit diesem Buch erneut nachgekommen.

English

After publishing two essential books for the Shotokan world, Kousaku Yokota presents his third work, *Shotokan Transcendence*, getting to the heart of today's karate.

Karate has inspired the creation of new forms while conquering the world as a martial art, a sport, and a political issue. Therefore, it has to be taken as the fundament of the persisting interest in and the broad variety of martial arts. But there has been criticism coming from several directions, and karate's new forms are not always appreciated. The discourse about its historical as well as its pragmatic authenticity is constantly being threatened by institutional turf wars.

Today karate offers many people steadiness and recognition, a possibility for athletic exercise, and interhuman relations. With this many ascriptions resulting from transcultural flows, they are almost impossible to set right. With his first two books, Yokota offered an important chance to deal with these old myths by asking questions that remain unpopular within the karate world even today, especially within Shotokan discourse.

Shotokan Transcendence takes the next step, pointing to the issues that are not obvious from the start. The book bridges the gap which practitioners of traditional martial arts are currently facing. This gap is a result of the way karate was taught, especially outside Japan. Yokota might shed new light on the karate of former idols such Masatoshi Nakayama and Tetsuhiko Asai. Asai in particular used to invite us to overcome the institutional limitations existing within the context of Shotokan. Kousaku Yokota followed that invitation with his new book.

FOREWORD

By Philipp Surkov

Country Representative, ASAI Germany

Göttingen, Germany

Born in St. Petersburg, Russia

О Ёкоте сенсее я узнал случайно, когда один знакомый посоветовал мне почитать несколько его статей в интернете. Эти статьи побудили меня, впервые с тех пор, как я начал заниматься каратэ, подумать самостоятельно. Вскоре я узнал, что Ёкота сенсей очень активен в социальных сетях, продолжает писать статьи и даже выпустил, к тому времени первую, книгу "Мифы Шотокана" (*Shotokan Myths*). Купив книгу без колебаний, я поглотил её и решил связаться с этим человеком, чтобы предложить ему заняться переводом его статьей. Я твёрдо уверен в том, что его идеи важны для каждого ученика каратэ, не только в Шотокане, и что они должны быть широко распространены на разных языках. Ёкота сенсей относится ко всем культурам с открытой душой и уважением. Доказательству тому служит факт, что на данный момент его статьи публикуются на восьми языках и всё больше добровольных переводчиков присоединяются к команде. Он считает дальнейшую глобализацию каратэ очень важной, так как искусства и энтузиазм объединяют людей.

В перечень его знаний входят все стили каратэ, а также кобудо, анатомия, психология и многое другое. Его манера письма легко понятна и иногда вызывающа, так как он хочет побудить читателя задуматься над кое-какими догматами, которые были привиты ему тренировкой. Его вторая книга "Загадки Шотокана" (*Shotokan Mysteries*) написана в той же манере и также входит в число моих книг. Вскоре после её публикации он решил создать собственную всемирную организацию АСАИ (ASAI · Asai Shotokan Association International), чтобы содействовать распространению стиля каратэ его учителя, легендарного Тетсухико Асая, в его полной и неизменной форме. В то время, как я пишу эти строки, АСАИ уже насчитывает сподвижников из более чем 30-ти стран. Из-за того, что тенденции к политическим разборкам и денежной прибыли большинства организаций каратэ меня тревожили, я долгое время отказывался вступать в какую либо из тех, что были предоставлены моему выбору. Однако я вступил в АСАИ, так как для меня она является молодым, свежим голосом в мире каратэ, борющимся старыми моральными качествами, но новыми методами за его идеал: Возврат к настоящему Будо.

В его третьей книге "Трансцендентальность Шотокана" (*Shotokan Transcendence*) Ёкота сенсей пишет, с одной стороны о внутренних механизмах человеческого тела, с другой стороны, как подразумевает название книги, о духовных и психологических аспектах боевых искусств. Как и в других своих книгах, он пишет о вещах, которые большинство учителей или забывают объяснить ученикам, или сами же не знают о них. Он относится к восьмому правилу Фунакоси сенсея из его Нидзю Куна "Каратэ-До не заканчивается за порогом додзё" очень серьёзно и показывает читателю на примерах, вроде бритья, или вождения машины, как вписать повышенную тренировкой каратэ внимательность (помимо прочих умений) в повседневную жизнь. Как человек, очень интересующийся психологией человека и работающий с техникой осознанности, я хотел бы подтвердить, что это очень важные темы, особенно в наше время, когда всё больше людей теряют идеалы и самосознание. Эту книгу не только стоит прочитать самому, но и поделиться ей со своими друзьями, которые возможно даже не занимаются каратэ.

English

I heard of Yokota Sensei by chance when an acquaintance of mine pointed me to some of his articles on the Internet. These articles encouraged me to think for myself for the first time since I began practicing karate. Soon I discovered that Yokota Sensei was very active in social networks, continued to write articles and had published, up to that point, his first book, *Shotokan Myths*. I bought the book without hesitating, devoured it and decided to contact this man to suggest translating his articles. I am of the firm conviction that his ideas are important for every karate practitioner, not only those of Shotokan, and that they should be widely spread in different languages. Yokota Sensei is openhearted and respectful toward all cultures. Proof of that is the fact that his articles are published in eight languages, and more voluntary translators are joining the team. He attaches great importance to further globalizing karate since art and passion connect people.

His knowledge extends to all karate styles, as well as *kobudo*, anatomy, psychology and more. His writing style is easy to read and sometimes provoking since he wants the reader to start questioning some of the dogmata he was trained into. His second book, *Shotokan Mysteries*, is written with the same style and is also a part of my book collection. Soon after publishing it he decided to create his own worldwide karate organization, ASAI (Asai Shotokan Association International), to promote his teacher's, the legendary Tetsuhiko Asai's, karate style in its pure and unaltered form. As I write these lines, ASAI has members from over thirty countries already. Since the political and profit-oriented tendencies in most organizations bothered me, I was reluctant to join any of the given options for a long time. I joined ASAI, though, since for me it is like a young, fresh voice within the karate world, fighting with old values but new methods for its ideal: the return to true *budo*.

In his third book, *Shotokan Transcendence*, Yokota Sensei elaborates, on the one hand, on the inner mechanics of the human body and, on the other hand, covers, as the title suggests, the spiritual and psychological side of martial arts. As in the other books, he writes about things that most teachers either forget to explain to their pupils or don't know of themselves. He is taking Funakoshi Sensei's eighth rule from the *Niju Kun*, "Karate goes beyond the dojo," very seriously as he is showing the reader, with examples like shaving or driving a car, how he can implement the mindfulness (among other skills) he learns from karate in his daily life. As someone who is very interested in the human psyche and works with the art of mindfulness, I can confirm that these topics are very important, especially in our time when more and more people lose their values and self-awareness. It is worth it not only to read this book for oneself but also to share it with friends who might not even practice karate.

FOREWORD

By Julien Soriano

Shotokan Yudansha

Member, Byakkokan Dojo

San Jose, California, USA

Born in Aix en Provence, France

Le Karaté Shotokan n'est pas un simple art martial. C'est un mode de vie, une pensée, une philosophie. Dans ses 2 premiers livres *Shotokan Myths* et *Shotokan Mysteries*, Kousaku Yokota partageait des aspects fondamentaux mais peu intuitifs pour la majeure du grand public ainsi que pour le plus assidus des karatékas.

L'expertise technique et spirituelle que Maître Yokota explique dans ses ouvrages, est une source d'inspiration inimaginable et inépuisable surtout dans la société actuelle dans laquelle nous vivons. Ce troisième opus dans la série *Shotokan* ne déroge pas à la règle et la richesse de son contenu n'a pas de prix pour tout passionné de Karaté.

Certes certains concepts peuvent paraître abstraits et difficiles à appliquer selon votre degrés de familiarité avec le sujet. Cependant - et c'est ici que la valeur d'un tel livre prend toute sa dimension - les sujets abordés peuvent être mis en pratique pour tout individu quelque soit son niveau.

Nous avons la chance que Maître Yokota non seulement partage son savoir et son expertise pour notre bénéfice mais mette à notre disposition toute cette connaissance d'une valeur inestimable dans des livres que nous pourrons consulter à tout moment. Ainsi, l'heritage du Karaté de Maître Asai peut perdurer.

English

Shotokan karate is not just a martial art. It's a lifestyle, a way of thinking, a philosophy. In his first two books, *Shotokan Myths* and *Shotokan Mysteries*, Kousaku Yokota shared concepts that are fundamental but not intuitive for most of the general public as well as for most of the most seasoned karate practitioners.

The technical and spiritual expertise shared by Master Yokota in his books is inspirational, especially in today's society in which we live. This third installment in the *Shotokan* series is no exception to the rule, and the richness of its content is priceless for any avid karate student or master.

However, while some concepts may seem abstract and difficult to apply depending on your degree of familiarity with the subject, the value of such a book is undeniable. The topics can be put into practice for any individual at any level with the appropriate motivation.

We are fortunate that Sensei Yokota not only shares his wisdom and expertise for our benefit but also makes it available in books that we can consult at any time and for many years to come. So, the legacy of Master Asai's karate can be passed on.

FOREWORD

By Luca Levorato

Shotokan, Wado Ryu, and Uechi Ryu Practitioner

Los Angeles, California, USA

Born in Venice, Italy

Con la predominanza dell'aspetto sportivo nel mondo Shotokan, abbiamo perso o dimenticato certi importanti aspetti che rendono la nostra amata disciplina cosi' speciale. Un grazie di cuore a Shihan Yokota per aver riportato alla luce detti aspetti che arrichiscono la nostra quotidiana pratica.

English

With the predominance of the sport aspect in the Shotokan world, we have lost or forgotten some important principles that make our beloved art so special. My special thanks goes to Shihan Yokota for bringing to the surface such aspects that enrich our daily practice.

FOREWORD

By Michael Johnson, Ph.D.

Nanadan, President, ASAI

Chief Instructor, Sierra Shotokan

Grass Valley, California, USA

With this book, Shihan Yokota has now become a true scholar in the world of martial arts. A scholar is one who selflessly and tirelessly engages in advanced study in order to pass this knowledge on to others. He has done just that. He indeed is a tireless researcher and chronicler. His numerous articles, blog entries, media presentations, seminars, and coauthored *kata* texts are examples of his productivity and passion for *budo* arts. As we all know, *Shotokan Transcendence* is his third text. In *Shotokan Myths*, he began his journey into the once forbidden answers to the mysteries of Shotokan. He continued this journey in *Shotokan Mysteries* and expanded upon the many unanswered questions and nuances of Shotokan.

Now, in *Shotokan Transcendence*, with the assistance of Shihan Yokota, we look "beyond" our everyday training regimen. We are asked in a very pragmatic way to examine and study our approach to *kata*, our everyday and common physical movements, concepts of self-defense, *budo* philosophy, cultural diversity, foundation percepts, and much more.

I can remember my first years in karate over forty-six years ago. I, like many of us, had many questions regarding history, technique, styles, the meaning of a *kata*, and so on. We never asked, and we were told to just "do" and not ask. Well, a lot has changed from those early days, and it is with the assistance of Shihan Yokota that these barriers have been broken and much has been shared.

The reader will begin to recognize very early that Shihan Yokota's style is very much Socratic in nature. He asks the reader over and over to examine his own perceptions, style, definitions, and reasons regarding the many subjects that he addresses. In short, he challenges the reader to look within. I have been his student for over thirty years, and I can attest that this honest and straightforward approach will challenge and push the practitioner to get much more from his training regimen, both physically and mentally.

Without question, this text is a valuable addition to any *karateka*'s library. It can also be read over and over again, and the reader will gain new knowledge and a new perspective each time.

PREFACE
初めに

My first two books, *Shotokan Myths* and *Shotokan Mysteries*, were published in 2010 and 2013, respectively. It is my great pleasure to report that these books received much highly positive feedback from the readers. Let me share with you two such reviews from the Amazon website.

> Shihan Yokota has done it again, but this time even better! His new book, *Shotokan Mysteries*, is a welcome sequel to *Shotokan Myths* and provides a wealth of information to illuminate the deepest recesses of Shotokan karate.

> When I knew about this book I got excited and needed to buy it due to the very good impression from the excellent *Shotokan Myths* written previously by the same author. And after reading *Shotokan Mysteries*, my expectations were fully satisfied, or even exceeded.

My search continued. In the third book, I started with a simple question: "Why is Heian Shodan not symmetrical?" To answer this simple question, I had to explain a unique part of the Japanese culture as well as a hidden requirement for our *kata* by the ancient karate masters.

Next, I decided to look into the reasons why we must preserve our *kata*. We consider our *kata* very important, but no one in the past has explained it scientifically or from a kinesiological perspective.

Then, I realized that many people are missing the important yet not too visible side of self-defense. I felt that it was the right time to explain another invisible subject, ki. It is something we all talk about and say is important, yet it has not been explained with easy words that everyone can understand. The reader will also find in this book the importance of the muscles that are not visible (core muscles) and the backbone.

I hope this third book, *Shotokan Transcendence*, will not disappoint the readers. I chose the word *transcendence* for the book title because I have been feeling keenly that we need to go beyond what is being taught in the Shotokan teachings. The last precept of Master Funakoshi's *Niju Kun* is to "always think deeply and be creative." It will bring me great pleasure if this book helps you to think more deeply and be more creative.

Musashi Miyamoto, a famous samurai, said that martial artists need to "perceive that which cannot be seen with the eye." I hope this book will give the reader some hints to help perceive the beauty and wisdom of the Shotokan teachings that may not be easily visible.

It is my sincere wish that we go beyond in our karate journey so that we can reach the next goal.

CONTENTS

CHAPTER ONE
第一章

A SMALL MYSTERY OF HEIAN SHODAN
平安初段の小さな謎とは

This is about a small mystery that some Western instructors have wondered about in the past, so I want to share my thoughts on this unique point in Heian Shodan (平安初段).

The question is the fourth movement, *jodan tate kentsui uchi*. No, I am not talking about its *bunkai*. The question is why we do not have this technique after the first *gedan barai*. In other words, some of these Western instructors thought an identical technique of *jodan kentsui uchi* was missing between move number 1, left *gedan barai*, and number 2, right *chudan oi zuki*. By having this technique here, Heian Shodan would become truly symmetrical and complete, wouldn't it? So, was this technique forgotten or taken out by mistake? Let us check the old textbook, Funakoshi's *Karate Do Kyohan* (空手道教範). I am sure you will find the same result; this "missing" technique is not there. Let us check Pin'an Nidan (our Heian Shodan) in Shito Ryu (糸東流) and Shorin Ryu (少林流). I find that the technique in question is not there either. We must conclude that this *kata* was created that way by Master Anko Itosu (糸洲安恒, 1831–1915) in the late nineteenth century. If this is the case, then there is a bigger puzzle. Why did he purposely skip or neglect a technique there and make this *kata* unbalanced? A hint is the key word of *symmetry*. This is a very Western concept of what is beautiful, correct, or complete. On the other hand, in Japan, believe it or not, we consider it totally opposite.

The Japanese people do not consider symmetry and perfectly balanced geometry correct or beautiful. They even consider them wrong and ugly. I know most readers will have an issue with my statement and perhaps disagree with it.

Let me show you a few examples.

One of the Japanese arts that have been exported to the world is that of ikebana (生け花), the art of flower arrangement. The photo to the right is not a diagram of *kata enbusen*. Would you be-

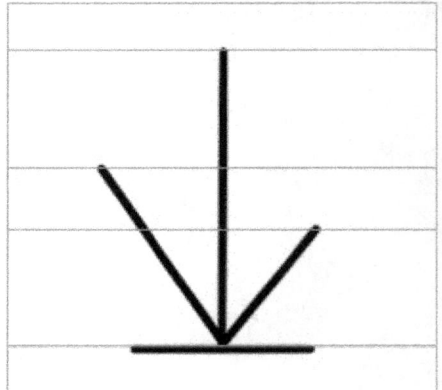

lieve this is from an ikebana textbook? It is to show the basic structure of the flowers or how they should look when they are arranged. The photo to the right shows an example of an actual flower arrangement, and you can see that the arranger has used an off-balance and asymmetrical format as instructed in the textbook. I do not know anything about ikebana and I have never taken any lessons, but I can explain to you why this must be this way as I know the Japanese mentality and sense of beauty. We know that nothing in nature and nothing natural in this world is symmetrical. In other words, anything that is symmetrical is artificial, which the Japanese consider imperfect and not pretty. Ikebana, flower arrangement, is an artificial decoration using something from nature, flowers. Of course, the flowers themselves are beautiful, and the flower arrangement, the artificial deed, must not destroy or decrease that beauty. To keep the beauty of the flowers, the Japanese choose to arrange them in an off-balance and asymmetrical way. Does that make sense?

Here is another example. Take a look at the teacups below. Another famous Japanese art is *chanoyu* (茶の湯), the traditional tea ceremony.

The photo below left is a teacup used in *sado* (茶道). See how the shape is purposely uneven, not round, and far from symmetrical? Even the design and coloring look almost as if they were done with some errors. I do not have the price list on this, but I am sure it is as expensive as, if not more expensive than,

the perfectly shaped Royal Worcester teacup shown in the photo next to it.

The concept of beauty is the same. We cherish what is natural and not ar-tificial or perfectly shaped. I am not comparing the beauty here or who is right or better (whether Japanese or Westerners). I am simply showing you the dif-ferent concept of the Japanese, which is deeply embedded in their hearts and even in their lifestyle.

Here are two photos of kimono, the traditional clothing for Japanese men and women. Though these clothes are not too popular anymore in normal life in Japan, as they used to be, many people still find special occasions to wear them. In Latin America, many people call a karate uniform a *kimono*, but this is an incorrect use of the word. If you wish to use a Japanese word for it, then it should be called a *karategi* or simply a *gi*. Regardless, the kimono pictured to the left has a design of a tree with its flowers in full bloom. The flowers on the left and right sleeves are designed differently, as you can see. Then, look at the design of the other kimono, the photo on the right. The imbalance or contrast between left and right is obviously very significant. I be-lieve this concept is quite different from the fashion of the Western world, particularly with regard to the clothing of the general public.

Interestingly, the *ukiyoe* (浮世絵) artists of the Edo period (sev-enteenth- and eighteenth-century Japan), such as Utamaro (歌麿) and Sharaku (写楽), had much influence on the Western artists who are classified as the impressionists of the nineteenth cen-tury. Some of these famous painters include Monet, Renoir, Cézanne, Matisse, Pissarro, Van Gogh, and many more. The academic painting method was to

draw as accurately as the object was perceived by the painter, but the impressionists "violated" the rules as they put more emphasis on the feelings and im-

pressions they got from the real objects and scenes (compare the styles shown
above). I assume these painters came to realize that it was impossible to copy
reality perfectly with their brushes. Japanese artists knew this for many centuries, and they perfected their impressionist painting style in the Edo period.

I could go on and show you many more examples from Japanese culture,
but let me share with you only a few more examples that are much bigger than
a flower arrangement or a teacup. When you visit Japan, many of you wish to
visit some exotic Shinto shrines as they look very Japanese, and the pictures
of yourself in a *gi* in front of a shrine look great (though Japanese visitors may
not appreciate it). Almost all of you are visiting not to pray but just to marvel
at the beauty of the structure and maybe the famous *a-un* (阿吽) statues. I
would say this is a perfect example of showing the concept of yin and yang.
A-un refers to an inhalation (阿) and exhalation (吽) of breathing. The term is
also used in Shinto and Buddhist architecture to describe the paired statues

common in Japanese religious settings, the *komainu* (狛犬), or guardian dogs, shown on the left of the previous page, and the *Nio* (仁王) shown on the right.

The concept of *a-un* is very interesting and deep. If you wish to learn more, read on this subject on *Wikipedia*: http://en.wikipedia.org/wiki/A-un.

The concept of imbalance or asymmetry extends to the concept of building a large structure, such as a shrine. Below is a blueprint of a shrine that was built more than half a century ago (photo left). The main part of the building is symmetrical, but you can tell the building as a whole is not as you take a look at the structures that extend to both sides of the main part. The right structure is completely different from that of the left. Let's take a look at a blueprint of a church and see how it is planned to be built. To the right is one from Saint Thomas More Church in Darien, Connecticut. I thought it was an interesting coincidence that the Japanese shrine's name is *Dairen*, and the location of the church is in the town of Darien, Connecticut. The similarity certainly stops there. If you can find the original photo on the web, you can expand the blueprint of the church. Even from the photo below, you can see that it is beautifully symmetrical. The right side structure is almost a perfect copy of the left and vice versa. The only difference is probably the restrooms (the one on the left being the men's and the one on the right being the women's).

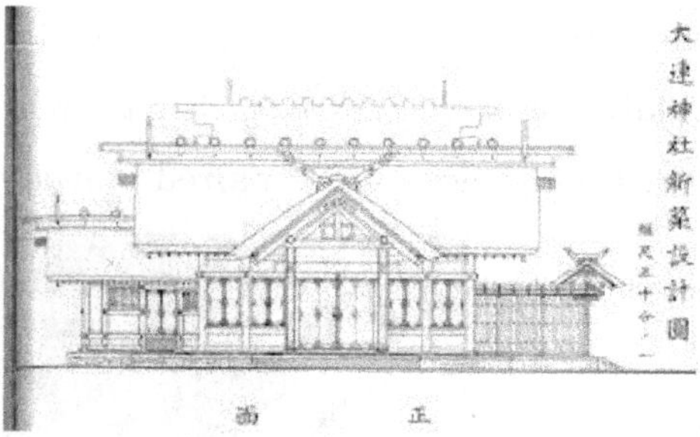

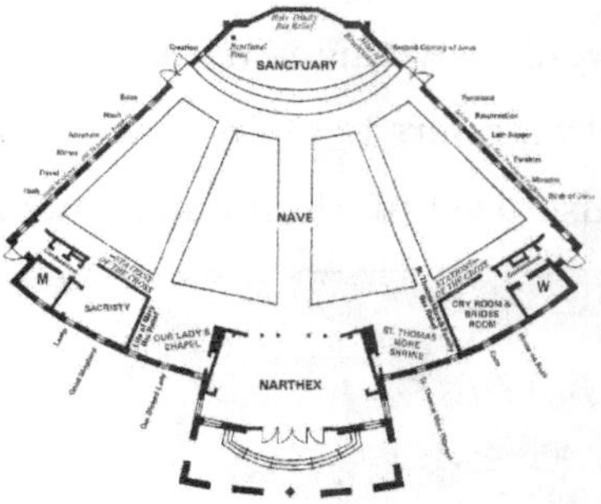

Now, do you agree with my conclusion that the imperfection of Heian *kata* was done on purpose?

I can almost feel how Itosu felt when he created Heian Shodan (originally

Nidan) more than a hundred years ago. It would have been a very boring *kata* if it did not have that one particular technique, *jodan kentsui uchi*. In other words, that move was a little spice to this *kata*. In fact, if you examine Heian closely, you will find that some of the key techniques are practiced only on one side (for instance, *chudan nukite* in Nidan, which was originally Shodan). You will find this not only in Heian but in all *kata*. You may want to review all the *kata* you know from this perspective, and you will discover that none of them are perfectly symmetrical. You would probably think, *OK, I understand the concept of the beauty by the Japanese people, but this is karate* kata. *Shouldn't the* kata *be designed so that we can practice these techniques on both sides?*

This is true, isn't it? Your puzzled thought is understandable, but the Okinawan masters had the answer. Master Itosu and other masters created *kata* to be asymmetrical on purpose to remind us that students must practice *gyaku kata* (逆形), mirror image. Unfortunately, the practice of *gyaku kata* has not been exercised by all Shotokan (松濤館) dojo. In my dojo, all brown belts are required to practice Heian as a *gyaku kata*, and one of those *kata* will be required at their *kyu* exam. I also ask the black belts in my dojo to practice the *gyaku kata* of all sixteen Shotokan *kata*. Tekki (鉄騎) and Gyaku Heian Shodan may not be too challenging, but try Bassai Dai (抜塞大) or Kanku Dai (観空大) as a mirror image. If practicing *gyaku kata* is not a part of your training syllabus, wouldn't you want to include at least Heian as a *gyaku kata* and get the most out of these *kata*?

CHAPTER TWO
第二章

SHIKO DACHI, A FORGOTTEN STANCE?
四股立ちは忘却されたのか？

Have you ever used *shiko dachi* (四股立ち) in your *kihon* or *kata*? If you are a Shotokan practitioner, I assume you have not. Do we find this stance in our *kata*? No, and as a result, we do not use this stance in our *kihon*. Haven't you ever thought it was sort of strange? I did. No one, as far as I know, has ever bothered to explain if there is any good reason why. If *shiko dachi* was there from the start, what happened to it? Isn't it an interesting question, and wouldn't you like to find out? Let us investigate together and try to find the answers.

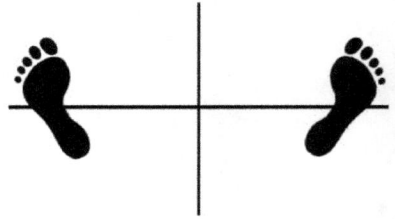

First, we need to look at Shotokan history by reviewing the textbooks. I always refer to two of the Shotokan classics: Funakoshi's *Karate Do Kyohan* (Neptune Publications Incorporated, 2005) and Nakayama's *Dynamic Karate* (Kodansha, 1966). I believe these two books are the foundation of Shotokan karate and the best references. I have a copied Japanese version of *Karate Do Kyohan* (空手道教範 [Kobunsha, 1935]), but for our discussion, I will use the translated version, which was translated by Harumi Suzuki-Johnson.

In Chapter 3 of *Karate Do Kyohan*, pages 22 and 23, Funakoshi lists seven stances, namely, *heisoku dachi, hachiji dachi, teiji dachi, zenkutsu dachi, kokutsu dachi, neko ashi dachi,* and *kiba dachi*. He states, "There are seven general stances." I am a little surprised by the incomplete nature of the list as it misses some very popular and important stances, such as *musubi dachi, fudo* (or *sochin*) *dachi, hangetsu dachi, tsuru ashi dachi, sanchin dachi,* and *kosa dachi,* to name a few. So, it is not a surprise that *shiko dachi* did not make the list. I will explain extensively why *shiko dachi* did not make it as a popular or key stance in Shotokan later in this chapter.

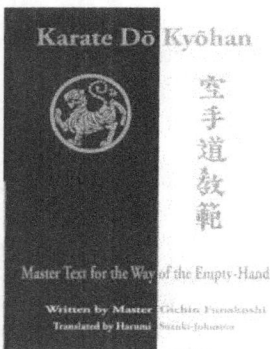

How about with *Dynamic Karate*? Its Chapter One is "Stance and Posture." On page 27, *shiko da-*

chi is listed among other key stances, such as *kiba dachi* and *fudo dachi*. Then, on page 37, *shiko dachi* is shown again by occupying the entire page with a photo and some explanation. However, the explanation by Masatoshi Nakayama (中山正敏, 1913–1987) is very short: "This stance is just like the straddle-leg stance except that the feet are turned outward at an angle of 45 degrees and the hips are lower. A plumb line dropped from the center of the knees would hit a

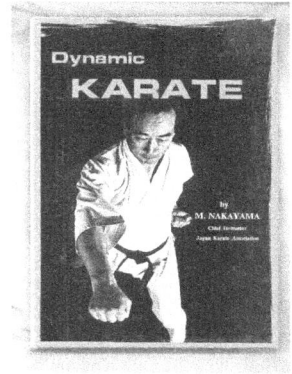

point midway between the feet." That is all. It does not say why it is included and how it is used. It is introduced twice, but you would wonder, *Why bother?* I will share my understanding regarding this subject toward the end of this chapter.

Now, let's look at the other styles and see if they use *shiko dachi*. It may be a surprise to some readers that this stance is a very popular stance. It is found in many *kata* from other styles. Probably the most representative one is Seienchin, which is one of the *shitei kata* in mixed-style tournaments such as those sanctioned by the WKF, the WUKF, and the WKC. This *kata* is one of the *kihon kata* practiced by the Naha Te (那覇手) styles, such as Goju Ryu (剛柔流) and Uechi Ryu (上地流) as well as Shito Ryu and Kyokushinkai (極真会).

Here is a URL for a video of Seienchin performed by a Shito Ryu competitor: https://www.youtube.com/watch?v=tDqOFQveOc8.

Here you can see that this *kata* is really based on *shiko dachi*. Though I am not familiar with the details of the Naha Te *kata*, I know *shiko dachi* is so popular that it is included in almost all *kata* (e.g., Seipai, Saifa, Gekisai, Sanseiru, Seisan, Suparinpei, etc.), and *kiba dachi,* on the other hand, is not used in any of them. It is almost like a mirror image of Shotokan. How interesting.

So, let's get back to the fundamental question: why do we not have *shiko dachi* in our *kata*? First, we must all remember the following fact. When Gichin Funako-shi (船越義珍, 1868–1957) learned his karate on Oki-nawa in the late nineteenth century, the Okinawan sensei had not needed to use any specific terms for the stances and techniques. The only terms they had were the names of the *kata*. An Okinawan instructor had only one or two students. The sensei showed the tech-niques with his body and did not give any explanation or need to assign terms to the different techniques. He would say, "Watch this *kata*," or, "Do this technique like this." My assumption is that Funakoshi was taught the *kata* but did not have the distinction between *kiba dachi* and *shiko dachi*. Thus, I assume he probably allowed both stances: *kiba dachi* and an open-toed stance (*shiko dachi*). He might have considered it as a relaxed ver-sion of *kiba dachi* when one could not do a tight *kiba dachi*. To have a perfect *kiba dachi*, you really have to pull your toes in and increase the inner muscle tension in the thighs. I am sure you have experienced that as soon as you relax your legs, your toes point out easily. In fact, look at Funakoshi's stance (photo above left). This is from Tekki, and his stance is definitely not a strict *kiba da-chi* as we know it. I'd say this is much closer to *shiko dachi*. Some people try to give him the excuse that he was old and could not hold a good *kiba dachi*. But, I think that is very disrespectful to Funakoshi Sensei as he was only in his fif-ties in this photo, so he was certainly not old. So, in the old Shotokan training, I assume he allowed *shiko dachi* as well as *kiba dachi* in different *kata*.

We no longer practice this stance. Was this stance considered an unneces-sary or even a bad stance? As I pointed out above, Funakoshi himself used *shiko dachi* in Tekki, and I assume he did in other *kata*, such as Jion, Jutte, and Gankaku. Thus, I do not think Funakoshi considered the open-toed stance *shiko dachi* to be unnecessary or bad. I am sure Funakoshi taught this stance to Nakayama because the latter added this stance in his book.

Was it purposely dropped from or changed in the Shotokan syllabus? I believe so. You would naturally wonder why. Let us investigate together.

You must know the history of early Shotokan, particularly before World War II, to understand what has happened to the karate Funakoshi originally brought from Okinawa. He started to teach karate in Tokyo in 1922, when he was fifty-four years old. He was not the first Okinawan to officially bring karate to mainland Japan. In fact, Choki Motobu (本部朝基, 1870–1944 [photo left]) moved to Osaka, Japan, in 1921. His karate level was excellent, and he was very agile, which earned him the nickname *Motobu no Saru*, or "Motobu the Monkey." His existence was almost unknown for three reasons: (1) he could not speak Japanese and had no influential connections in Japan; (2) he was reputed by some to have been a violent and crude street fighter; and (3) his training was so severe that not too many students could last and continue to be his followers.

Funakoshi moved to Tokyo in 1922 and, to his credit, he could speak Japanese and was lucky to make a good connection with Jigoro Kano (嘉納治五郎, 1860–1938), the founder of judo. So, he was the only karate sensei in Tokyo then, but soon other Okinawan masters started to arrive in Japan. The most notable one was Kenwa Mabuni (摩文仁賢和, 1889–1952 [photo right]), the founder of Shito Ryu. He visited Tokyo in 1928 and decided to move to Osaka in 1929 to live there. Funakoshi's profession was that of a school teacher, and he was not a full-time karate practitioner when he lived in Okinawa. He learned from two teachers, Azato and Itosu, but he learned only the Shuri Te (首里手) style of Okinawan karate.

Mabuni, on the other hand, was a policeman, so he
had a lot of time to practice karate. In fact, he trained
almost full time and had two famous teachers: Itosu
from Shuri Te and Higaonna from Naha Te. So, Mabuni
learned Okinawan karate in a very comprehensive way.
As a result, he became legendary for his encyclopedic
knowledge of *kata* and their *bunkai* applications. By the
time he arrived in Japan, he was regarded as the fore-
most authority on Okinawan karate, *bunkai*, and karate history.

So, what had happened here with Funakoshi's teaching in Tokyo? Most of
his students were young students from various universities in Tokyo. However,
some adults from other martial arts, such as judo, jujutsu (Otsuka, who later
founded Wado Ryu), and kenjutsu (Shimoda and Konishi, who later founded
Shindo Jinen Ryu), also joined to learn karate on a professional level. So far
so good. However, he faced his first problem as the students became more advanced and wanted to know a lot more about *bunkai* and practice *kumite*. Ever
since he arrived in Tokyo, he had only taught *kata* and some *bunkai* explanation, but there were no *kihon* or *kumite*. He was very adamant about sticking
to only *kata* training and prohibited any *jiyu kumite*. In fact, he resigned from
one of the university karate clubs as he found the students there were secretly
practicing *jiyu kumite*. It is clearly recorded that many of his students were
very dissatisfied with the way Funakoshi trained them.

Mabuni, on the other hand, had a different attitude. He welcomed *jiyu kumite* and went as far as practicing full-contact karate using protectors (photo
above left). Many university students became curious about Mabuni, so they,
along with Otsuka and Konishi, visited Mabuni's dojo to learn about *kumite*.
Moreover, Mabuni knew more advanced Shuri Te *kata*, such as Unsu, Sochin,
Gojushiho, etc.

So, what did this mean to Funakoshi? In the thirties, he faced serious
competition from Motobu, Mabuni, and other Okinawan masters. What did he

do? Now what we have to put the spotlight on is Funakoshi's talented son, Gigo (or Yoshitaka) Funakoshi (船越義豪, 1906–1945), who moved to Japan with his father when he was only seventeen (1923). By 1930, Funakoshi Senior was over sixty years old while his son was twenty-four years young but had been practicing karate for more than twelve years under his father (starting his official training when he was twelve years old). Gigo was not an expert yet, but he proved to be very talented and strong.

In 1934, Funakoshi's number-one assistant instructor, Shimoda, died from an illness. After this, Gigo took over the position and started to have a strong influence on Shotokan karate, which his father had brought from Okinawa. Funakoshi Senior believed the basic sixteen *kata*, or even fewer, were enough. Gigo disagreed as he was young and wanted to learn more *kata*. What did he do? He went back to Okinawa to learn more *kata* and *bunkai*. He also visited his "competitor," Mabuni, to learn more Shuri Te *kata*. Gigo is also credited with many different kicking techniques, such as *mawashi geri*, *ushiro geri*, and *yoko kekomi*. He also believed in low stances (photo above right) and did not like high stances, such as *neko ashi dachi* and *sanchin dachi*. I also assume Gigo changed from moving techniques using high stances to still ones with low stances, such as *kiba dachi* and *zenkutsu dachi*.

You also know it is easier to move if the toes are pointed outward like in *shiko dachi*. So, when you do the body shifting from one *kiba dachi* to another in a *kata* such as Jion or Jutte, your stance becomes more like *shiko dachi*. Gigo Funakoshi also shows that this is true (see above photo). I know your instructor will tell you to pull your toes in. You've also realized that you can squat more deeply if your toes are pointing out, and it is extremely difficult to lower your hips when you have a perfect *kiba dachi*. This is natural when you consider how your leg bones and hip joints are constructed.

So, Gigo thought *shiko dachi* was a defective *kiba dachi* and decided to drop it from the syllabus. In all *kata*, the stance was limited to *kiba dachi*, and *shiko dachi* was discouraged or even prohibited.

We know that Gigo had a big influence on both Shigeru Egami (江上茂, 1912–1981), the founder of Shotokai, and Nakayama, one of the key organizers of the JKA, until Gigo's passing in 1945 at the very young age of thirty-nine. It is very interesting that two organizations developed their own techniques, including the stances, so differently in such a short period of time despite having the same origin (Funakoshi Sr. and Jr.). I will not go into the details of the differences between Shotokai and JKA Shotokan in this chapter, but look at the *shiko dachi* in Shotokai (photo left). The feet are pointing outward on a straight line, which is very unique, and it does not look like the stance we know. Try to stand this way. You will find it is very unbalanced, and you will not be able to keep the stance if you are pushed from the front or the back. A quick lateral body shifting is possible, but I am not sure why they chose this stance and called it *shiko dachi*. Maybe a Shotokai practitioner can enlighten us.

So, where did *shiko dachi* originate? Many readers may already know that it is from sumo (相撲), traditional Japanese wrestling. The exact period of origin is not known, but it can be traced back to the sixth century or earlier. Prior to becoming a professional sport in the Edo period (seventeenth century), sumo was originally performed on the grounds of a shrine or temple. It is still popular in Japan and is broadcast on TV as a fifteen-day tournament that happens six times per year. It keeps some old traditions, such as throwing salt in the ring, which is supposed to purify the ground. Women are barred from the ring, so all of the workers have to be male. There is a controversy regarding this policy at the sumo association, and many people, both men and women, have protested, but so far this policy has not been changed.

There's more on sumo here if you are interested: http://en.wikipedia.org/wiki/Sumo.

The most popular stance in sumo is called *shiko dachi* (photo right), in which one can take a very deep squatting position. The rule for winning or losing in sumo is pretty simple. A sumo wrestler must either push his opponent out of the ring (4.55-meter diameter) or force him to touch the ground with any part of his body besides the bottoms of his feet. In ancient times, they were allowed to hit and kick even if it could hurt the opponent. One famous story tells that one sumo wrestler killed the other by kicking him, and he won. Nowadays these two techniques are prohibited; however, an open-hand slapping is still permitted, though it is not considered an honorable technique in modern sumo.

In fact, *shiko dachi* is very popular in Japan because many athletic coaches believe this is the best stance to strengthen players' legs for their own athletic activities.

For example, you will find warm-up and leg exercises using *shiko dachi* in basketball training (photo below left) and soccer practice (below right). I do not need to show photos of judo and Western wrestling practitioners, but they also engage in exercises such as deep squats using *shiko dachi.*

I want to show one more example. One of the most popular sports in Japan is baseball. The photo below left shows the kind of exercises Japanese high school baseball team members do.

The photo on the right shows the famous Japanese baseball player Ichiro Suzuki (鈴木一朗, 1973–), who now plays for the New York Yankees. One of the exercises he does on the field is his stretch using a wide *shiko dachi* as seen in the photo. So, what happened to *shiko dachi* when Nakayama formed the JKA in the mid-twentieth century?

Nakayama was not only highly trained in karate; he was also aware of modern science and the medical aspect of the human body. He knew the great benefit one could get from training in *shiko dachi*. To show respect for Funakoshi, he did not change the stance from *kiba dachi* to *shiko dachi*. What he did was to keep this stance for leg exercises. We practice deep squats often in our training in Japan (photo right) to strengthen our legs. Nakayama added *shiko dachi* in his book *Dynamic Karate*. Unfortunately, he failed to put an explanation as to how this stance should be used and what the

benefits were in his book. I wonder if this omission was intentional or not. Regardless, as a consequence, I am afraid that the importance and the necessity of *shiko dachi* have not been relayed or taught enough to Western Shotokan practitioners.

Then, what are the benefits of *shiko dachi* specifically? There are two major benefits that I can quickly point out. One of them is the training of the inner muscles that connect the thighs to the pelvis. Training these muscles is not easy, but it is extremely important for karate. I have mentioned these muscles in the chapters on weight training and relaxation. I will not explain these muscles again, but I ask you instead to read those chapters so that you can get the full story behind this subject. One thing you can do is slow and deep squats using a wide *shiko dachi*. You will feel the tightening or the tiring of the muscles that are located inside your thighs. You may wonder if the same muscles can be trained by using *kiba dachi*. Try deep squats using *kiba dachi*. Where do you feel the pressure? Do you not feel it mostly on the front of the thighs? Of course, you will use the hamstrings and the rear muscles (gluteus maximus), too, but you will use the quadriceps the most. In *shiko dachi*, even though you will use the quadriceps, you will mainly use the inner muscles, such as the adductor longus, adductor magnus, etc. (see the illustration to the right). I have mentioned in the past that strengthening these muscles is very important to any athletic activity, including karate. The exercise of the inner muscles cannot be maximized if you practice with *kiba dachi* alone.

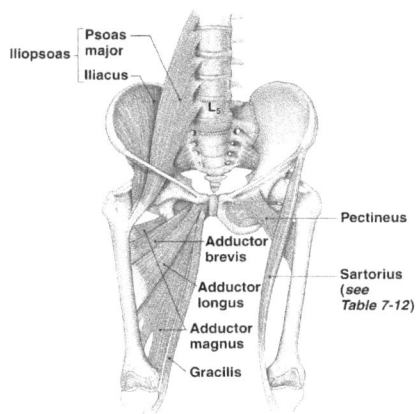

Psoas major
Iliopsoas
Iliacus
L₅
Pectineus
Adductor brevis
Adductor longus
Sartorius (see Table 7-12)
Adductor magnus
Gracilis

(c) The Iliopsoas muscle and the adductor group

The second benefit of *shiko dachi* is its mobility. In Seienchin *kata*, you will see that the practitioner moves not only sideways (back and forth) from *shiko dachi* but also toward the front in an interesting way. Of course, you can do this with *kiba dachi*, but you can do it more easily with *shiko dachi* as your feet are pointing outward, which makes the stance less restricted. So, *kiba dachi* gives you a more solid or stable stance, but *shiko dachi* can be more mobile. You can keep a steady *kiba dachi* when you are in that position without any body shifting. However, when you shift your body, regardless of whether you move toward the left or right in *kihon* or *kata* such as Tekki, Jion, Jutte, etc., your feet will naturally open up, though your instructors will yell at you to keep your feet parallel.

Then, the natural question may be this: if this stance is so beneficial, why didn't Nakayama explain more about *shiko dachi*? My answer will be only my guess. I did not hear the explanation directly from Nakayama when I met him before his passing. However, I know that he had a great respect for both Funakoshi Senior and Junior. He was sort of sandwiched between these two instructors. So, he believed *shiko dachi* could be used in the *kata* interchangeably with *kiba dachi*, but he did not want to put it in writing. He only added this stance in the *tachikata* (stances) list without any explanation. He intended to explain the importance to his students in person, and I know that he had done so with the JKA instructors. However, this omission in his book resulted in one of the Shotokan mysteries.

To supplement Shotokan *kata*, Hirokazu Kanazawa (金澤弘和, 1931–) practiced Seienchin himself. I am sure one of the reasons for practicing this *kata* was to get familiar with *shiko dachi*. I suspect his followers must be aware of or practice *shiko dachi kata*, such as Seienchin.

Here is a video of Kanazawa performing Seienchin: https://www.youtube.com/watch?v=0U7KPaiZJ08.

In addition, I can assume Hidetaka Nishiyama (西山英峻 1928–2008) also felt the need for *shiko dachi* in our *kata*. This is not widely known outside his organization, but he created a *kata* called *Kitei*, in which *shiko dachi* is included.

Here is a sample video of this *kata*: https://www.youtube.com/watch?v=McVf2bTvqSs#t=13.

If this is the case, the big question is this: why didn't the information that *shiko dachi* is important spread more to the Western world? I cannot answer that question, but I feel strongly that it is very unfortunate. I wish to recommend that the reader add this to the standard training syllabus now so that more Shotokan practitioners can enjoy the benefits of this excellent stance.

Conclusion

Shiko dachi was a part of the original Shotokan karate that was brought from Okinawa by Gichin Funakoshi. *Shiko dachi* was used almost interchangeably with *kiba dachi* in the Shotokan *kata* in the early twentieth century.

Gichin's son Gigo, being physically strong, emphasized the strong and steady stances, such as low *zenkutsu dachi* and low *kiba dachi*. He discarded or ignored the high stances, which included not only *neko ashi dachi* and *sanchin dachi* but also *shiko dachi* as it is less stable (though more mobile) than *kiba dachi*.

Nakayama, knowing the benefits of *shiko dachi*, kept the stance in the syllabus. However, he did not push this stance as he decided to keep all *kiba dachi* in the JKA *kata*. He wanted to use it only in the leg exercises (mostly squats). He failed to write about its use and benefits in his famous book *Dynamic Karate*. We do not know if the omission was intentional or unintentional. Unfortunately, this resulted in the general omission of this stance from standard Shotokan training.

Shiko-Dachi

If you have a problem executing a strict *kiba dachi* because of lack of flexibility or some other reason, now you can relax. You no longer need to feel depressed or discouraged. You found that *shiko dachi* is an excellent stance, and it is more flexible than *kiba dachi*. I will not go so far as to recommend replacing *kiba dachi* with *shiko dachi* in our *kata* as I believe the *kiba dachi* requirements of the inner thigh tension and butt tucking are important and necessary for us to master. Since you can use *shiko dachi* in your Shotokan *kata*, such as Jion and Jutte, learning a Naha Te *kata*, such as Seienchin, is not necessary. However, the inclusion of exercises using *shiko dachi* in both *kihon* and *hojo undo* (補助運動) is, I conclude, critically important and necessary for all Shotokan karate practitioners to improve their karate.

CHAPTER THREE
第三章

GYAKU ZUKI AND THE
REAR HEEL RELATIONSHIP
逆突きと後ろ足の踵の関係は？

I am sure you agree that *gyaku zuki* (逆突き) is one of the most popular punching techniques in karate, and I do not need to explain how it is done. This technique is also the most effective one to get a *waza ari* (技有り) in a *kumite* tournament.

Whether this technique is indeed an effective technique from a *bujutsu* (武術) perspective is another story, but we are not focusing on this point in this chapter. The subject or the key point I want to bring to your attention is the heel of the rear foot. Look at the photo on the right. It shows a practitioner (left) giving a *gyaku zuki* counter while simultaneously blocking a *mawashi geri* (回し蹴り). It is a nicely taken photo, but you'll also notice that the person's rear heel (right foot) is off the ground. In fact, his entire right foot is off the ground. So, the question is this: is this a good *gyaku zuki*, or is it an imperfect *gyaku zuki*? Honestly, I have received this same question from many practitioners (including some senior ones) in the past. Should the heel be on the ground while we do *gyaku zuki*? Why do they ask this question? It is because in some cases, it is almost impossible to keep the heel down, but we were consistently taught to keep the heel down while doing *gyaku zuki*. We have never been given the explanation that it is OK (or even better) to lift the rear heel up in some cases. This subject is not a very difficult one if you understand the kinesiology behind the technique. Unfortunately, many instructors are unable to do so because they did not learn it from their sensei, and most of them have not questioned this. I will present the explanation so that this subject will no longer be a mystery.

A disparity starts from the textbooks. One example, Nakayama's *Dynamic Karate*, shows a photo of Nakayama (中山) himself doing *gyaku*

zuki in *zenkutsu* position. The photo at the bottom of the previous page is an excellent one as it shows four clips merged together to illustrate how it should be done from the *yoi* (用意, 'ready') position to the final execution of *gyaku zuki*. As you can see, the heel of the rear foot (right leg) is firmly on the floor. Other instructional photos, such as the one on the right of world famous Kanazawa (金澤) Senior, show the same. In other words, the heel of the rear foot is sol-idly planted on the ground. Interestingly, the textbook for Masutatsu Oyama's (大山倍達, 1923–1994) style, Kyokushinkai full-contact karate, shows the same posture for *gyaku zuki* (photo left). I practiced Kyo-kushin for a year and watched many of their tournaments, but interestingly, I have never seen a knock-down resulting from a *gyaku zuki*, especially with the form shown below by Mas Oyama. OK, so it is commonly agreed that both of our feet must be firmly on the ground when a *gyaku zuki* is executed from a stationary stance.

When you did *gyaku zuki* as you were going through *kihon*, did your sen-sei tell you to keep your heel down? I suspect if your heel was up, your sen-sei might have come behind you and tapped it with his *shinai* (竹刀, 'bamboo sword') or stepped on your ankle to force it down. If this is the case, we have been ingrained through repeated *kihon* exercises with the notion that a correct *gyaku zuki* must have the rear foot flat on the ground. By the way, I am not dis-puting this point. I fully agree that a correct *gyaku zuki* in a stance where the body weight is either equal or is distributed greater than fifty percent toward the rear leg must be done this way. However, a proper explanation about this has not been provided to many practitioners. Anyway, let me continue with the discussion. The frustration begins as soon as you practice *gyaku zuki kihon* as you step forward. You do not encounter this problem when you do this punch in a stable *zenkutsu dachi*. However, I suspect that you experienced a problem when you did it in a quick-step forward combination. Your heel "had" to come up. You probably said to yourself, *Hey, my ankle is not as flexible as Kanazawa's, so I cannot help it*. Or, you just gave up. You do not need to blame your flexibility (or lack thereof) or give up. You will see why as I explain this further.

After *kihon*, you normally practice *kumite*. When you are a beginning student, you start with either *gohon* or *sanbon kumite*. The defender will step back three or five times in those *yakusoku kumite* (約束組手, 'prearranged sparring' or 'agreed sparring') drills, and he does *age uke* then uses *gyaku zuki* as a counter (photo left). Most of the time you do well with this *uke* and *gyaku zuki* combination as long as you do not lean forward to punch. If your distance is correct, you can do a good *gyaku zuki* counter with your heel firmly planted on the ground. If it happens to be up, your sensei will come again and tap your heel or press it down with his foot. Sensei will explain to you that a big and strong hip rotation is important to generate power. In order to do this, the rear foot must be flat on the floor to give solid support to the *jiku ashi* (軸足, 'supporting leg'). You have no issue with this and you practice this way hundreds of times. It works in *ippon kumite* (一本組手) and most of the time in *jiyu ippon kumite* (自由一本組手, 'semifree sparring') if the exercise is a basic *jiyu ippon* (自由一本) and not a complex one, such as *nihon gaeshi* (二本返し), in which the attacker counters the defender's counterattack.

Then, you will get to the point of total frustration when you get involved in *jiyu kumite* (自由組手, 'free sparring') and *shiai kumite* (試合組手, 'tournament sparring'). The two photos below show the typical technique used to get a point. It is estimated more than sixty percent of *kumite* points are scored with a *gyaku zuki* technique. So, what is the problem here?

In *jiyu kumite* and *shiai kumite*, you find that it is almost impossible to keep the rear heel down. Why? It is because you are most likely moving forward as you execute this technique. This means your front leg becomes the *jiku ashi* ('supporting leg'), and less weight is distributed to the rear leg. If fact, you will be punching mostly on one leg (the supporting one).

In the sixties and seventies, your *gyaku zuki* would not receive a *waza ari* if your heel was up. That would be considered a poor technique. This also happened in the U.S. in the early days. Johnson Sensei of Sierra Shotokan Dojo shared his experience in his training at Nishiyama (西山) Dojo in LA. Here is his recollection:

> Nishiyama would continually state the power came from the heel as it met the floor. Even in advanced training he would stress the point that one could not score without the foot firmly planted. He would state that the technique was not deserving of a point unless grounded.

In the photo below, Hideo Ochi (越智秀男, 1940–), who is pictured on the right, is delivering a *gyaku zuki* to his opponent as Nakayama serves as chief judge at the 1967 All Japan Championship. I wonder if Nakayama gave Ochi a *waza ari*. It would be interesting if any of the German readers could ask if Ochi Sensei remembers this *shiai*.

The rules have changed since the JKA joined the WUKO in 1981, and a quick reverse punch can now score a point (*waza ari*) even if your rear heel is off the ground. If the timing is perfect, then you may even get an *ippon*. Whether the heel is on the ground or not has become a nonissue in a tournament setting. I agree that it is not a mistake or an error if your rear heel comes off the ground in a particular situation, which I will explain later. I am aware that many practitioners and their sensei would still consider this a flaw, however. You may ask if delivering the strike from a one-legged stance would decrease its power as it is not leveraging from a solid stance based on both feet. Surprisingly, it would not if your body were moving forward. The lost power from not having a stable stance is more than compensated for by the energy of the body moving forward. In addition, your stance gets longer than a standard *zenkutsu dachi* as you can see in the above photos, and this makes it more natural to support the rear leg with the ball of the foot rather than trying to keep the entire foot on the ground. So, in a quick action, especially when you are shifting forward, it is OK and even better to shift your weight to your front leg and deliver the *gyaku zuki* with your forward-moving momentum. At that time, your back heel will not be on the ground, and that is not a problem.

Then, is it wrong if your rear foot is firmly planted on the ground in *kumite*? No, that is the way it should be when you are stepping back. When you step back, your body weight is naturally going backward, and more weight is distributed to the rear leg, so it is much easier to keep the rear foot down and deliver the power from the rear leg, which happens to be the *jiku ashi*. The same mechanism can be experienced when you do a *mae ashi mae geri* and use it as a counter. It can be a very powerful kick even though you may be stepping back.

Conclusion

For a *sen no sen* application, your gravity will be moving forward, and most of your body weight will be shifted to your front leg. In this case, your rear foot will be lifted as you execute a *gyaku zuki*. This is a very natural thing, and it is not a problem.

On the other hand, in a *go no sen* situation, you will most likely use the rear leg as the supporting leg; thus, it is better to have the entire foot firmly placed on the ground. This application, from a mechanical perspective, will take more time to deliver a *gyaku zuki*, so it will require a lot of timing practice to overcome this "slowness." Also, one must learn how to capture the moment in order to reverse the mechanical disadvantage of *go no sen*.

The conclusion is that both delivery methods are correct. Hopefully, this chapter can put your mind at ease, and you will no longer worry much about your rear heel while practicing *gyaku zuki*.

CHAPTER FOUR
第四章

WHAT PART OF YOUR FOOT DO YOU USE WHEN YOU TURN?
回転の時には足のどこを中心にして回るか？

In the past, I have received questions from
many people, in essence, asking something
like this: "When we turn, what part of our
foot should we use as a pivot point?" They
specifically ask if they should turn on the
ball or on the heel of the foot when they
rotate the body. We all know it is very im-

portant for all karate practitioners to be able to turn quickly and smoothly. In
fact, I consider this an independent technique. Here I will attempt to provide
a short chapter to describe my understanding of this technique. I would like to
hear back from the readers as to whether they agree or disagree.

Now, before we talk about turning, we need to pay attention to and understand two important concepts: (1) center of mass and (2) center of gravity. They
are different, but for the purposes of our discussion, they are interchangeable.
I will quote some parts from *Wikipedia* to explain the definitions of the center
of mass and the center of gravity.

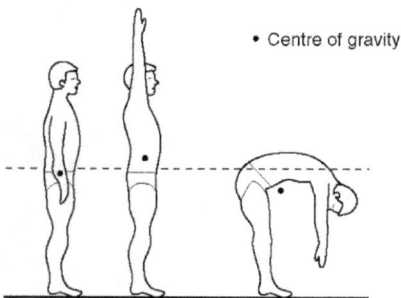

In physics, the center of mass of a distribution
of mass in space is the unique point where the
weighted relative position of the distributed
mass sums to zero. The distribution of mass is
balanced around the center of mass and the average of the weighted position coordinates of the
distributed mass defines its coordinates. Calcu-
lations in mechanics are simplified when formu-
lated with respect to the center of mass. In the case of a single rigid body, the center
of mass is fixed in relation to the body, and if the body has uniform density, it will
be located at the centroid. The center of mass may be located outside the physical
body, as is sometimes the case for hollow or open-shaped objects, such as a horse-
shoe.

Regarding center of gravity, *Wikipedia* also states that

in physics, a center of gravity of a material body is a point that may be used for a summary description of gravitational interactions. In a uniform gravitational field, the center of mass serves as the center of gravity. This is a very good approximation for smaller bodies near the surface of Earth, so there is no practical need to distinguish "center of gravity" from "center of mass" in most applications, such as engineering and medicine.

So, I have a choice of terms, and I will use the term *center of gravity* in my discussion. To shift the body even to take a simple step, you need to shift the center of gravity. Believe it or not, you cannot simply stand up from a chair if your head is prevented from shifting forward. Try the following experiment. Have your friend sit up straight in a chair, and you place the tip of your index finger on his forehead, preventing him from leaning forward. Challenge him to stand up and see if he can. You will find that it is impossible for him to stand up normally until you let go of his forehead.

First of all, do you know exactly how your foot is constructed? If you don't know how your racing car is constructed, you will never be a world-class race car driver. The principle is the same with our body, though our body construction is much more complex and precise than a race car or even the most advanced jet fighter. Here is an illustration of our foot. You probably had some

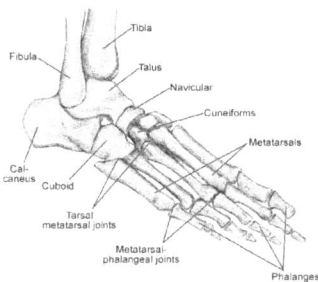

idea that the bone structure of your foot looked like this. However, I suspect you have not paid close attention to the finer details of the bones that make up this precise mechanism called the *foot*. The human foot and ankle is a complex mechanical structure containing twenty-six (26) bones, thirty-three (33) joints, nineteen

(19) muscles and tendons, and one hundred seven (107) ligaments. The precise numbers are not important. What is important is that you realize that your foot is made up of a very complex construction. The muscles and ligaments surround these bones so that you can make numerous precise movements with your foot. One of those precise movements is walking. It is not possible to do a simple walk without the harmonious workings of the muscles, tendons, and ligaments of our feet. I am always so impressed and truly thankful whenever I study the mechanism of our body. Don't you agree that it is really the work of a genius and that our body, indeed, is a masterpiece?

Believe it or not, the first humanlike robot that could walk like us became possible only in the year 2000. A robot called ASIMO (Advanced Step in Innovative Mobility, photo right) was designed by Honda and introduced in October 2000. I wanted to mention this because the precise mechanism of bipedal walking is unique. Bipedal walking (and leaving the front legs or hands free) was necessary for the Homo sapiens to set themselves apart from the other primates. Bipedal walking can be easily perceived as a simple body movement, but it is incredibly complex and difficult for a machine to imitate. I have covered this topic in one of my previous books, so I will not repeat it here. The point I want to emphasize is that we must never think lightly of the abilities of our body that were given to us.

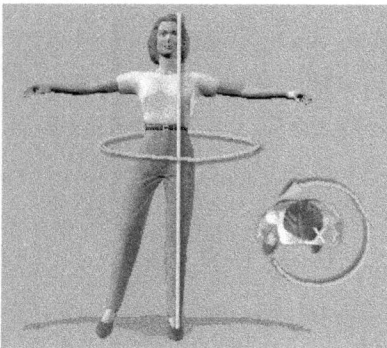

Back to the original question: what part of our foot do we use when we turn? My answer is that there are basically three different ways to turn, and the part you use will depend on the situation. One situation is a turn in position or an in-place body rotation (photo left). In this case, you will line up the center of gravity through one leg (the pivot

leg), the hips, the torso, the shoulder area, and all the way up to the center of
your head. If you can line up all these parts as straight as possible, then your
turn can be smooth and fast. This turn is often used in dancing, figure skat-
ing, and gymnastics, to name a few. A body rotation technique can be found in
various karate *kata*, such as Kanku Dai, Gankaku, Junro Yondan, etc. If you
are familiar with these *kata*, you will know which parts of the *kata* require the
rotation. In these cases, you need to use the part that is directly below your
shin bones. Again, take a look at the illustration of the foot (below).

You may have a misconception that the lower legs are made up of only one bone. Actually,
there are two bones: the tibia and the fibula.
There are two so that you can rotate and move
your foot just the same as we have two bones
in our forearm to move and rotate our hand.
As shown in the illustration, they are not posi-

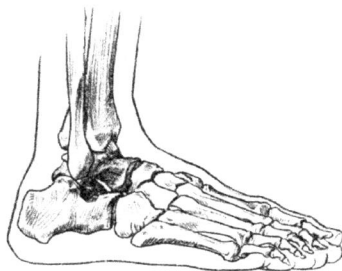

tioned in the center of your foot. The ankle is the point where these bones are
connected, and we now know that the ankle is located nearer to the heel than
to the toes. We also notice that there is an arch and that the foot is concave
in the midsection. This means there is no protruding point to turn on directly
under the ankle. This makes it extremely difficult to turn at the best point, i.e.,
directly underneath the ankle. So, most dancers use the heel part or the contact point of the bone called the *calcaneus*. However, it is difficult to keep balance in the case of complex or multiple rotation, so as an alternative, they can
use the ball of the foot, the area underneath the third joints of the toes. Turn-

ing on the ball of the foot requires much more
precision, but we have the tools (joints and
muscles) to control the turn and balance with
the front part of the foot. The area of the ball
of the foot is rather large (illustration left).

Senior professional dancers use only one spot—the best spot is under the middle toe, though some may choose the spot under the big toe because it is usually the strongest toe—but inexperienced dancers may float the spinning point across the foot, which results in a slower and more poorly balanced turn.

For an in-place rotation, the area underneath the ankle is the most recommended spot as it gives the best balance for the simple rotations that are found in most *kata*. However, we have discussed and pointed out that this method is the most challenging and most difficult one to use. I propose to the reader that the best alternative is to use the heel. I recommend that the reader try to bring the turning point as close as possible to the spot directly under the ankle.

Sorry to have started with the most challenging technique. There are two other turning methods that are easier, and you are probably already doing them. To turn as you are moving forward (as in the left *gedan barai* move after the first *kiai* in Heian Shodan, for instance), you will want to use the ball of the foot. As I have mentioned previously, the center of the foot (third joint) is the best specific pivot point on the foot. In a standard Shotokan dojo, I suspect that you were taught to keep your body upright when you shift. As you advanced in your training, you might have found that it is better to lean your upper body slightly toward the direction of your turn. By doing this, you found that you could move faster and more smoothly. The first move of Bassai Dai may be an excellent example. Even though an excessive degree of incline would be counterproductive, you do want to incline slightly toward the turning side. Let's take the example of the move I mentioned above in Heian Shodan after the first *kiai*. You want to incline slightly to the right as you turn from the right *zenkutsu* to left *zenkutsu gedan barai*. In this turn, you may use a different part of your foot. It is still the ball of the foot area but may be closer to or right at the edge of the right foot. This requirement is the same with any other physical activities, such as football. See the player in the photo to the right? He is inclining to his right as he makes a quick right turn. If you

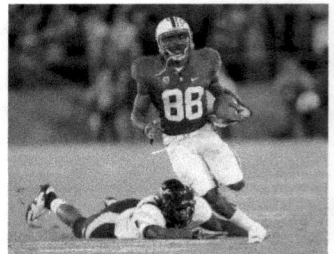

could expand the right foot area of the photo, you could see that the runner is turning on the ball of the right foot on the side of the little toe. Football has much more complex running and foot movement requirements in its execution than the karate *kata*. Thus, we cannot adopt the steep incline they use, but the concept or objective of quick and smooth turning is the same. This will require a fine alignment of your foot to the leg bones. You may ask why. Take a look at

the illustration of the leg bones (left). Just to line up the leg, you have to pay attention first to the hip joint, then to the knee joint and ankle, and then to the numerous other small joints in your foot. This is only in your leg. For the entire body, you have the joints of many other parts, but for our discussion, let's focus on the leg area alone.

What is the key to a good turn? Simply put, the fewer joints you use in your body alignment, the more easily you can keep balance and turn smoothly. It does not take a rocket scientist to understand this logic. Let's look at a top, which is something you probably played with when you were a child. It can demonstrate a beautiful spin or rotation. As you know, the axis is straight and short. But, imagine if the axis were long and made of several pieces that were not lined up. How about if those pieces were not firmly connected? Can such a top spin? That is almost how our body is constructed. Now you know why it is difficult for us to spin. Look at the illustration of the foot again and you can see that the bone structure of the heel area is much simpler. The front area that covers the toes is much more complex. This is natural as we normally walk

forward and less frequently walk backward. Then, can we do a turn using the heel part of our foot while moving forward? Yes, it is possible, so you can. You may feel more stable by turning on the heel; however, turning on the ball of the foot will give you a much faster

turn.

Then, what is the third method? You can easily guess that it is a turn as you move backward. Remember the third move of Heian Shodan? After the second move (right *chudan oi zuki*), you step back with your right leg and turn 180 degrees to do a right *zenkutsu dachi* with a right *gedan barai*. What part of your foot do you think you will use to do this turn? Yes, this was an easy question. Most of you probably said, "Heel." As you step back, it is natural and easy to shift the center of gravity to the heel. One word of caution on the use of the heel. The heel area (calcaneus) is a simple bone structure, and it is a blessing in one way. At the same time, however, it can make your turn more challenging. The heel area is simple, being without joints and ligaments. This means you are unable to do the fine tuning that can be done with the ball of the foot. To master turning on the heel area, you will need to do a lot of practicing and learn how to be stable and well balanced during the turn.

To be able to execute the most effective body turns in your karate, you need to be able to manage all three different turning methods. A turn may look simple, but the mechanism to deliver the most effective turn certainly is not. A good turn is important in all athletic games. So, I'm sure you'll agree that it is also extremely important in karate if you happen to be serious about perfecting your technique. Shotokan is labeled as a linear or straight-movement martial art. If we look at our *kihon*, it may appear linear, but when we observe expert Shotokan practitioners perform, we all witness that our karate is filled with circular techniques and body movements. Asai Ryu (浅井流) karate is a great example of this as it adopts many *tenshin* (転身, 'body rotation') techniques.

Did I give you too much information? Maybe so, but it will make more sense to you as you read this chapter several times. You may think this information was written only for advanced practitioners or instructors. Even though I want instructors to read the information written here, I was also thinking of beginning- and intermediate-level practitioners. It is better for beginners to learn the techniques correctly at the early stage of their training. As you know, once you form a habit, it will be very difficult to change or correct later. The ability to turn correctly is much more important than most practitioners give it credit for. When you play basketball, football, or tennis, isn't a superior turning ability important and even necessary? If so, then why not in karate? To improve your karate, you know that you need to practice all three *K* elements: *kihon*, (基本), *kata* (形), and *kumite* (組手). Regardless of which *K* element you may be practicing, one of the key requirements for your improvement is that you master the technique of perfect turning.

CHAPTER FIVE
第五章

THE REASONS WHY WE MUST PRESERVE OUR KATA
形を保存しないといけない理由とは

Discussing the concept of *kata* (形) is a huge task and an extremely complex one because it involves almost every aspect of the physical and mental functions. I am always amazed by the beauty of the design and capability of the human being. I cannot help but to thank God for the masterpiece He has created. Our body (physical and mental) is far more complex and precisely designed than any machine or mechanism we have been able to create.

Now, let us talk about *kata*. According to *Wikipedia*, *kata* is described as a Japanese word describing detailed choreographed patterns of movements practiced either solo or in pairs. The term *form* is used for the corresponding concept in non-Japanese martial arts in general.

Most readers already knew that much, but you may not know that the kanji for the word *kata* has not been agreed upon in Japan. The same reading is used for two kanji (形 and 型), but they have two different, albeit similar, meanings. The first kanji, 形, means 'form' or 'shape', and the second one, 型, means 'model', 'mold', or 'pattern'. So, the meaning of 形 is more general and describes the ambiguous concept of a form or shape. On the other hand, the meaning of 型 seems to be more specific as it refers to a mold to make a certain form or pattern. As I mentioned earlier, there is no consensus among Japanese karate styles and organizations. Different kanji are used depending on the style of karate, and even that is not a hundred percent accurate as these two kanji are used interchangeably. Here is the cover of the book *Karatedo Kata Kyohan* (photo left), published by Japan Karatedo Federation (JKF). They use 形, and Shotokan also tends to use this kanji. Another book (photo right), published

by Okinawa Goju Ryu, shows 型 in its title, *Karate no Kata*. Okinawan styles seem to prefer this kanji. This is historically interesting because pure Japanese martial arts, such as kenjutsu (the forerunner of kendo) and jujutsu (the forerunner of judo), use 形 for their *kata*. Okinawa definitely has a unique history and did not receive much cultural influence from mainland Japan until as late as the mid-nineteenth century. Therefore, the Okinawan people may have a different understanding or feeling about these kanji.

OK, that is enough with the kanji lesson. I assume that many readers will agree that *kata* is a very unique component of not only karate but also all Japanese martial arts, or *bujutsu* (武術). The training method of *kata* really separates *bujutsu* from sporting events and the Western fighting arts (e.g., boxing, wrestling, etc.). Now that you know this, why did the Japanese masters develop and adopt the concept of *kata*? What is the true purpose of *kata*? It is true that *kata* is a perfect training method when you are alone or when you do not have a training partner. With *kata*, you can train any time and almost any place. You can also train secretly if you want to keep your karate training confidential. All of these reasons seem like good enough reasons why the ancient masters created *kata*. However, some of you already know that they were not the real reasons. Training had to be alone even though some *kata* (those in jujutsu, for instance) were made for multiple practitioners to perform as *tori* and *uke*. There is a real secret to *bujutsu* and the depth of its teaching. I hope this chapter will help you to appreciate the wisdom of the past masters.

Let me explain why the Japanese masters of *bujutsu* believed in the necessity of *kata* (mostly solo performance). First of all, in order to start discussing this subject, we must understand the complexity of the mechanism of the body (including the mind) in the martial arts. In fact, this happens to be the most complex and demanding of all physical activities. I am not saying this because

I am a proud karate instructor. This is not a biased statement, and I will explain exactly what I am saying below. By the way, as far as I know, the theory I am going to present here has never been discussed or mentioned by any instructor in the past.

To illustrate the complexity of the physical/mental mechanism of *bujutsu*, I will compare it to some of the popular sports. In fact, I will list them from the simplest (mechanical) structure to the most complex (ending with *bujutsu*). A few sporting events, such as boxing, wrestling, fencing, and archery, originated from martial arts. Sporting events were invented and created for pleasure and leisure. To maximize pleasure, many of them take the form of competition. This is why we can put kendo, judo, and karate in the sports category. Those who want karate in the Olympics feel very comfortable with the idea, and those who are into *bujutsu* feel very unhappy with this recent movement, which did not succeed for the 2020 games.

Before I go further into the comparison, I want to stress the true intention of my action so that the reader will not misunderstand the point I will try to make. What I will present here is simply that the complexity of the physiological and mental mechanism of the martial arts is greater than that of sporting events. What I want to emphasize is that I am not looking down on the sports category nor claiming that *bujutsu* is better or more valuable than sporting events. Such comparison is futile and meaningless as these are two totally different animals. Let me restate that the comparison I present here is only from the perspective of mechanical structure (both physical and mental) and complexity, not from the perspective of value.

Hopefully, I have made myself clear on that point. Now I want to start with the simplest or easiest competition structure of sporting events. Good examples in this category may be track-and-field running and swimming competitions.

Let's take a hundred-meter sprint as the first example. In this event, you have only a few rules and requirements, such as reacting to the starting gun and staying in a given lane, but not too many more. With those rules, the only thing a competitor has to do is run as fast as he can. First of all, a competitor does not need to learn a new technique. Almost everyone knows how to run naturally, so what he needs to do is improve his running technique to go faster. What is most important here is that the other competitors not bother you or interfere with your running. If someone does this, then that runner will be disqualified immediately. In other words, in a normal track-and-field sprint event, a runner can focus all his attention on his running. These are the key factors that make this event the simplest event. This means the performance of the runner will mostly depend on the runner's natural talent. Of course, in order to run faster, he has to train his body, run a lot, and also improve his running style. However, the amount of new techniques he must learn or acquire is extremely small.

Swimming is a little more complex because the ability to swim is a learned or acquired skill unlike the ability to run, which is a given and is unnecessary to learn (of course, a toddler must learn this ability). In a swimming competition, there is little interaction between the swimmers, and the only objective is to swim as fast as you can or faster than any of the other competitors in the same race. Structurewise, this is pretty primitive, and you can see why I say it is the simplest.

Golf fits into this category. Though it involves hitting a ball and playing against opponents, the rules are the simplest. The ball is set on the ground and does not move. The opponents are quietly watching your performance and do not interactively play "with" you.

Though the rules are the simplest, I am not saying it is the easiest to play. If it were, no sponsor would pay millions of dollars to professional golfers.

The second level of complexity is an event that involves some interaction between the competitors. The simplest examples of this category include tennis, Ping-Pong, and badminton, where you play against only one opponent (I will talk about doubles later). You can easily see that the biggest difference from the previous category is that your opponent will directly affect and almost dictate your actions and reactions. In other words, if he hits a ball to the right side of the table or court, you have to run there to hit the ball back. If he hits high, then you have to reach high to hit the ball back. It gets more complex as the number of the players increases. Playing doubles is, of course, more complex than playing singles in Ping-Pong and tennis. On the same token, it gets more complex in baseball and volleyball. The events in this category share the similarity of having an offensive and a defensive team. However, baseball is simpler than volleyball as most of the interactions are between a pitcher and a batter. The rest of the players are basically standing still and waiting until the batter hits. Volleyball is a little more complex as the volleying, or hitting of the ball to each other, will continue as long as the ball stays in the air. Both of these have a rule that keeps all of your opponents in their court or off the field while your team is playing. Opponents are not allowed to come on to your court or field to disturb you.

Another rule we must pay attention to in baseball is that the offensive side is fixed. Until the pitcher throws the ball, the game does not start. Of course, there is a rule that limits the time to get ready, so the pitcher cannot spend one hour before throwing the ball. But, he can basically take his sweet ole time to get set before he throws the ball. This means that, though under stress, he will be able to prepare himself in the best possible condition for his attacking action (throwing the ball).

In this category, a more complex structure can be found in football (soccer) and
basketball. It is more complex because the
offensive and defensive sides are not fixed,
and they can switch very easily if the ball
is intercepted. Even though the players on
the opposing team cannot harm you intentionally, they can block or even tackle
you (in rugby), which means not only do you have to carry the ball, but you also
have to defend yourself by running away from or dodging the pursuing opponents. This is a huge key factor that makes the game faster, more unpredictable, more complex, and more challenging to play. Players must learn and acquire different kinds of techniques and more of them to play these ball games
than tennis and baseball. On the other hand, there still exist many rules that
keep the game fairly simple. Let me list a few. There is always only one ball
in play on the court or field. Can you imagine if there were two or three balls
in a basketball game? The goal or hoop belongs to one team, and you have to
get the ball to the other side. In basketball, a player cannot carry the ball as in
rugby. He has to dribble or pass it to one of his teammates. In rugby, a player
can carry the ball but he cannot throw it forward. Interestingly, the more rules
you have, the simpler the structure of the game becomes.

Once again, I am not saying all these ball games are inferior to the martial
arts or claiming it is easy to become a top player. For instance, in basketball
and volleyball, a player needs to be able to jump high, so those players are
definitely much better at jumping than the average martial artist. I am sure
most football and basketball players can run faster than most martial artists.
They may even have more stamina and possibly more endurance as they have
to run for many minutes in their game. These things are all true, but still the
difficulty and complexity of the game or competition structure are lesser than
those of *bujutsu*.

Now, the last category before *bujutsu* is martial arts-like sports. I want to

list boxing, kendo, judo, and sport karate
(both full-contact and noncontact karate)
and compare them to *bujutsu*. The martial
arts-like group has a much more complex
structure. Once a fight or a competition
starts, there is no offensive or defensive

side. After the bell or *hajime* command, your opponent will attack whenever
he can, and you will do the same. This means you will have to assume the offensive and defensive sides at the same time. Please note that this fact is the
key point that has a deep relationship to the creation and adoption of *kata*. I
will explain further on this later.

Out of the four events I have listed, boxing
and full-contact karate are probably the most
brutal as in these two events, the competitors
actually hit each other. The fear factor also
needs to be considered, and it is very important though oftentimes ignored. Though it is

a very interesting subject, I will not go into this at this time. Structurewise,
this group must perform under the most complex and challenging fighting or
competing conditions. However, they still have some rules, such as a time limit
and a fixed fighting ring or mat. And, the rules prohibit or limit some actions
for safety reasons. For instance, in boxing, you cannot use your legs for kicking.
In full-contact karate, for instance, punches to *jodan* or *gedan* are prohibited.
They certainly do not allow eye poking, kicking to the groin, hair pulling, bit-
ing, etc.

In the concept of *bujutsu*, there are no rules, and anything goes (though
there are some rules and limitations for *kumite* in the actual training). In *bujutsu* training, one must practice for all possible situations and scenarios. This
very fact or requirement puts martial arts into the most complex and demanding environment. Fighting time extends to 24 hours a day, 7 days a week, 365

days a year. Everywhere you go could turn into a fighting site, and everyone and everything you meet or see could be your opponent or enemy. In *bujutsu*, there is no clear separation of offensive and defensive sides. Oftentimes, you may have to perform both functions at the same time. Another big difference that makes *bujutsu* far more difficult is that there are an infinite number of situations and possibilities for attacking and defending. First, the physical characteristics of each opponent/enemy are all different. Attackers come in all sizes, and they may even have weapons in their hands. Unlike in a tournament, they may attack you from behind, or they may be hiding behind a door, a car, etc. Therefore, there could be millions of different *bunkai* situations.

Of course, their attacking techniques will be infinitely different, too. Most of them may punch (although almost never with a karate punch), and some opponents may be experienced street fighters or boxers. Some may swing a stick or a knife at you. Some may be under the influence of alcohol or drugs. I worked as a bouncer in a bar when I was training in Philadelphia many years ago, so I know a drunken man can be a monster. He does not feel pain and can be totally unpredictable. I have also fought against a group of thugs in a parking lot that was covered with snow. I was not smart as a *mawashi geri* came out of me naturally as one guy pulled his arms up to strike me. I was lucky that I did not slip and fall down. I could not knock him down with that kick as I was off-balance, but they gave up and ran away after realizing I was a karate practitioner. In your *bujutsu* training, these variable environments, situations, and requirements (both mental and physical) must be considered and also practiced accordingly. In essence, the no-rule fighting style of *bujutsu* creates the most complex and challenging situations and conditions you can have.

I have spent a lot of time and space explaining the levels of complexity in the fighting/competing structure of different physical activities. This was necessary before I could explain why *kata* is necessary. I am not sure if I was successful in making myself clear on this concept, but I needed to do this before I could dive into the real subject of *kata* and the learning processes that are intricately combined and associated with the physical and the mental.

So the big question is this: how can you practice in a way that is feasible for no-rule fighting?

Earlier I presented you with a long introduction to explain the different levels of complexity that are associated with the physical and mental requirements in various types of competitions or sporting events. I concluded that the requirements and the complexity of *bujutsu* are the greatest and most challenging. My explanation may not have been full or comprehensive enough, but I hope the reader can agree with the basic concept. Now I expect that you would ask, "OK, *bujutsu* may be the most complex physical activity, but what has this got to do with *kata*?" If you have not seen it yet, the key point is there, so I would like you to remember this clearly so that you will understand what I will explain next.

First, I need to start with another basic concept. There are at least three main requirements that uniquely separate martial artists from sports athletes.

One of the requirements is the development of the 24/7 fighting mind-set or attitude. This mind-set was a part of the daily life of all samurai in the Middle Ages. Modern-day policemen and soldiers might truly understand this requirement. Funakoshi left many of his teachings in his *Niju Kun* (二十訓). One *kun* states, "*Dojo nomi no karate to omou na*" (道場のみの空手と思うな), meaning 'karate training must not be considered only inside a dojo'. Another one is "*Danshi mon o izureba hyakuman no teki ari*" (男子門を出づれば百万の敵あり), meaning 'once you are out of the door of your house, you may encounter a million enemies'. He was telling us the mind-set of a samurai, which is also necessary for *bujutsu* karate. This mind-set, *zanshin* (残心), is very unique, and it requires some special training to develop this difficult skill, but we will not cover this in this chapter. One day I will

write about this interesting subject.

Another requirement is the fear factor. In karate, we are supposedly train-ing to master techniques to kill people. In our *kumite* training, your opponents are attacking you in order to knock you down or kill you. This feeling of fear (and how to overcome it) is needed for martial arts training. This is another big differentiation from sporting events as their main objective is to score a point, reach the goal faster, win a prize, etc., and ultimately to enjoy the event or race. By getting used to free sparring, one can overcome the fear somewhat, but that is only with another unarmed *karateka*. Besides, I have visited many dojo around the world and have found that the intensity in *kumite* is not that high in most of them. How will you overcome fear when you have to face an op-ponent with a knife or a gun? How about when you encounter a hijack situation with a guy with a gun who may be intending to fly the plane into a building? Are you going to watch and see what happens? Are you going to stand up and try to stop this guy even though you may be shot down? This is the kind of fear all *bujutsuka* must think about and be ready for. There are special training methods to overcome this level of fear, but here again, I will skip it and will include it in the longer version.

To explain about *kata*, we need to go deep into the third unique require-ment for *bujutsuka*, or martial artists. This is the serious necessity of learning and perfecting the techniques. Martial arts fighting means to kill or be killed. Therefore, your techniques must be excellent to survive in a fight. Any mistake could mean death for you. Now you tell me, "OK, I agree that martial artists have to seriously improve their techniques to prepare for a life-or-death fight. But, how can the necessity of learning the techniques be unique to martial artists? Even golfers have to practice their swings and putts." This is true, but there is a hidden agenda that is related to the training of the techniques. Some serious golfers may practice shadow swinging (i.e., swinging without hitting the ball), but I doubt too many amateurs need to do this since the necessity for this type of training is rather small. Let me explain why they do not need to practice the shadow swing too much. I have already mentioned that at the time when you are about to swing your golf club, no one will bother your form with any kind of disturbance, including talking in a loud voice. In fact, such an action is considered a foul. I am sure you have seen this at a major golf championship where an official gives some kind of sign to the audience (photo right), and they force you to keep quiet. Under this rule, no one around would push you or throw a punch at you. Therefore, golfers can focus their attention on only one thing: how to hit a still ball that is placed on a tee as perfectly as possible.

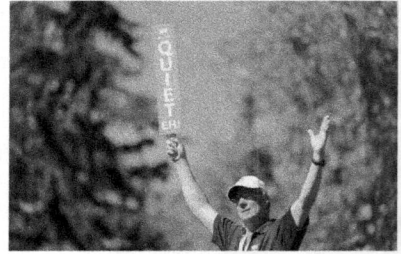

Let us look at our karate training and the area of *kumite*. Many instructors believe that in order to improve *kumite* (note: I am referring to *jiyu kumite* [自由組手], 'free sparring'), you have to do a lot of *kumite*. Some have even dropped *kata* on the basis that *kata* techniques do not work or cannot apply in *kumite*. I have seen a few instructors put white belts into *jiyu kumite*. One instructor insisted that it was a necessary thing for a white belt to learn these "natural" fighting techniques rather than the rigid and "unnatural" moves called *waza* (技, 'technique'). How wrong can they be! I felt sorry for the white belts, but they seemed to enjoy it (whatever it was).

So, what's wrong with this? Let's dig into this concept of learning *kumite* through doing *kumite* and see what it does. First, if you are a brown belt or above, I suspect you have done *kumite* before. Please recall how your techniques were in your *kumite*. Didn't you find it extremely difficult to deliver a clean or good technique in the fast exchanges of *kumite*? How were your combinations or the exchanges of attacks and blocks? Were they anything close to perfect? I suspect your answer would be no. I know it is almost impossible because your opponent will interfere by attacking, blocking, and doing other actions while you are trying to throw a technique. You cannot have the undisturbed conditions in *kumite* that a golfer can expect. Under these conditions, your "simple" technique becomes far from perfect. Your punch or kick may be blocked, or you may be off-balance, etc. Now, we are talking about one technique here. In an actual fight, there will be multiple techniques and maybe with multiple opponents.

You agree that when fighters are going full speed, it will be impossible for them to throw perfect or even decent techniques. The tech-

niques become sloppy unless you happen to be an expert in *jiyu kumite* already. I know you can deliver a technique in *kumite* to a degree, but can we really expect to practice the techniques in *kumite*? Your techniques are not perfect or even near perfect, so you would just be repeating those bad techniques. By this training method, you will continue to repeat sloppy techniques. And, what will result from this training method is that your sloppy techniques will become your best techniques. This is the concept I refer to: "the more you practice, the worse you get." Here is an example of a very poor *kumite* performance by black belts: https://www.facebook.com/photo.php?v=433968960035092.

By watching this, I hope you will agree that this person's techniques will not improve no matter how much more *kumite* he engages in. This is why I stated that one cannot train in karate (the most complex structural form) in the same manner found in golf (the simplest structural form). You now understand that we humans can normally focus on only one major physical or mental activity at a time. To be able to multitask, you need to have some special training. In *kumite*, a fighter's movements are only reactions.

Here is a famous comment Bruce Lee (李小龍, 1940–1973) made in one of his movies (I am sure many Lee fans remember this): "Don't think. Feel!" It sounded good and impressed fans of the movie, but he was only half-correct. If he were talking to an experienced practitioner, he would have been correct. But, in the movie, he was talking to a young boy who looked like a beginner

(photo right). As a martial art instructor, he was incorrect to give the boy such an order. In other words, it is the same thing as telling him, "Don't do *kihon kumite*. Do only *jiyu kumite*." It is true that there are many things you can learn from doing *jiyu kumite*, such as distance, timing, and body shifting. I hope you agree that *jiyu kumite* is not for the beginner and should be kept only for the advanced student (black belt). A beginning student must be taught to think all the time and monitor his movements as much as possible so he can learn the correct techniques. The ultimate stage, of course, is "feel," where your natural reaction (without thinking) is a nearly perfect or correct technique even in *jiyu kumite*. But, it will take many years for the beginner to get to that state, and he needs to seek out and engage in the proper training (i.e., a lot of *kihon kumite*, *kata*, and *kihon*) to get to that stage.

You may disagree that *jiyu kumite* is not the best training method to improve *kumite*. It is true that we could modify *jiyu kumite* to make it better as a training method. You could force the fighters to reduce the speed of all the techniques in *kumite* considerably so that they would move very slowly. In this way, they could give much more attention to their techniques. As they improved and got better at that particular slow speed, they would speed up gradually. This idea may sound good; however, I tried this myself and with my students many times. What happens—and you will find this out yourself if you try it—is that you cannot keep the motions slow for very long. The fighters may start with slow moves initially, but they will still have to react to each other's moves. Pretty soon both of them will end up going faster and faster. Consequently, their techniques get sloppy very soon, and it becomes a regular *jiyu kumite*. On the other hand, if you force them to move slowly all the time, then there is the frustration of not being able to practice at the faster speed. This is the catch-22 of practicing *kumite*.

It is true that there are other kinds of *kumite* training. Let's take a look at them. After Shotokan was brought to mainland Japan in the early twentieth century, *yakusoku* (約束, 'agreed') or *kihon* (基本, 'basic') *kumite* was invented. There are different kinds of *yaku-*

soku kumite, so let's take *jiyu ippon kumite*, which we call *free single attack*. This is an excellent training method, and I recommend it to any intermediate student and even to the *yudansha*. As you know, in this training menu, the attacking side can throw a technique without disturbance by his opponent. It is good for the defending side, as well, as he has much vital information, such as which technique the attacker is going to throw (*oi zuki*, *mae geri*, etc.), what area he will target (*jodan*, *chudan*, etc.), and the knowledge that the attacker will not (supposedly) engage in more than that one attack, i.e., he will not block the defender's counterattack, initiate a second attack, etc. There are many variations of *jiyu ippon kumite*, but unfortunately, at most dojo, I know they practice only one standard kind. Practicing only the standard *jiyu ippon kumite* is definitely not sufficient. However, I do not blame them. If you begin to expand the *jiyu ippon kumite*, you may end up with several hundreds of different kinds. This is the limitation of *jiyu ippon kumite*. The other *yakusoku kumite* are all good for beginning and intermediate students, but they are not sufficient. Thus, we conclude that there must be a different way of practicing to improve fighting skills.

Let me go back to golf as there is an interesting comparison between golf practice and karate training. When we talk about golf practice, most golfers think of a driving range. You get a bucketful of golf balls and you systematically hit them. Your main objective is to hit them as far as possible and in a straight line without hooking or slicing. Here you can find similarities to our *makiwara* (巻藁) practice. Both of them involve solo work, hitting a fixed/still

target, and having a fixed stance. Some of the objectives of *makiwara* training are also similar as you want to hit the target straight on and at maximum
power. Of course, there are many more objectives in *makiwara*, so it is a much
more complex training. We cannot equate it to practice on the driving range,
but I thought it was interesting to note those similarities.

So, the ancient masters realized that solo practice was necessary for *bujutsu* training because *bujutsu* was (and is) the most complex physical and mental
activity. Did the Okinawan masters invent *kumite* practice? No, they did not,
and you have already read why earlier in this chapter. All *kumite* training
syllabi were developed after karate was introduced into Japan in the early
twentieth century. Then, did they invent *kihon*? No, the *kihon* syllabi were also
developed and added to karate training in the early twentieth century. What
did they invent then? You know the answer. They invented *kata*. They also
practiced *bunkai*. As this chapter is getting long, I will not discuss why *kihon*
was not invented, but you can assume that the ancient masters believed *kata*
was sufficient.

Now, before we go much further into the explanation of *kata*, I need to
bring up another important concept. There are two types or ways of learning
technique that are necessary for the martial arts. As far as I know, this concept
has never been fully explained to the karate world in the past. Once you learn
this, it is not a difficult concept, but you realize it is an important one. The concept needs some explanation, and understanding this will be important when
we come to the objectives of *kata*, which will be discussed later.

Let us look at the detailed concepts.

Learning Process 1: Acquiring Technique

One learning objective for the *karateka* is the pure acquisition of a technique. As we all know, in karate, we must learn many basic techniques, such
as stances, punches, kicks, blocks, and many other skills. After learning the

single techniques separately, you need to go on and learn various combinations (the number of which is huge). The important point in this learning process is the word *acquire*. This is not only learning, knowing, and understanding how the techniques work but also acquiring them, which means the techniques must be a part of the body system. In other words, after having learned the correct techniques, one needs to be able to execute them as he wishes. Getting to this stage requires a large number of repetitions to ingrain those techniques into one's body system. We have already discussed that solo practice is needed in this process. During solo practice, a practitioner does not have anyone or anything to disturb his execution; thus, he can give a hundred percent of his attention to his performance. By doing this, he can get the maximum result in learning and acquiring the techniques.

Learning a technique by repetition is a well-known method, and all of us *karateka* have been doing this diligently. To learn all sports and new activities, you need to do some repetition, as well. Even to learn a small task that may involve only the hand or fingers, repetition is required. Here are a couple of examples. When you went to a Japanese restaurant for the first time, you could not handle the chopsticks well. You needed to practice using them. It was a new skill of finger coordination that you had to acquire. Have you ever experienced a situation in which you had to write with your opposite hand (e.g., the left hand if you are right handed)? It is a hand-and-wrist coordination that had to be transferred to the opposite side. In both cases, you will become capable after many repetitions. Of course, we can list all the sports activities as almost all of them need to be learned with some degree of repetition.

The ancient masters thought about the complex combinations and attempt-ed to simulate actual fighting situations or samples of fighting sequences. It is impossible to cover every technique and scenario no matter how long one *kata* may be. Therefore, they selected the most frequently used combinations in an attempt to make the best sample of the actual fighting. A student can practice this slowly at first to learn the correct techniques. Then, he will repeat this process until the techniques become a part of him.

For learning and improving single or simple combinations, I am sure you will agree that *kihon* training is best. I am sure the practitioners of the past broke a *kata* sequence down and repeated the same technique or techniques many times as we do in *kihon*. However, the standard *kihon* training was in-vented and introduced only after the introduction of karate into Japan. I will cover more on *kata* after the explanation of the second learning requirement.

Learning Process 2: Learning How to Use Those Base Techniques

I am sure the first one was easy to understand and well known to all. Here is the second one, which I feel has been ignored and missed by many *karateka* and instructors. It is the learning of how to use or apply the techniques in a real situation (i.e., a fight), and that, in and of itself, is a technique. This is extremely important, and I want to make sure that all readers, especially the instructors, understand this concept.

In the first process, the student learns how to punch, for example. After learning a base technique of how to throw a punch, it is still not enough to make it useful. To make it useful (effective), he must learn other critical skills (techniques), such as *maai* (間合い, 'distance'), accuracy (hitting the correct target), delivery of power, body shifting with the technique, and many more. For example, unless a person can shift or move to the correct distance in rela-tion to his opponent, his punch or kick will be ineffective no matter how fast or strong his attack may be. If he misses the target, then that technique is also ineffective. These skills (e.g., *maai*, accuracy, power delivery, body shifting, timing, etc.) are the additional techniques that are necessary to use or apply your base karate techniques.

This is a very important concept, and all instructors should understand this as it must be applied to their teaching. This is why Funakoshi Sensei encouraged students to strike a *makiwara* (the concept of the driving range as in golf).

The learning process is an interesting area. There are many things that even modern science has not been able to explain, and some parts of the learning process are among them. When we look at the learning process, we believe we learn only from many repetitions. For instance, it takes a lot of practice before you can use a pair of chopsticks. It is the same thing before you can type fast. There are many more, so I am sure you can easily come up with other cases. However, there are some things that require a knack (*kotsu* [骨], in Japanese) to master the skill. This is interesting, so let me give you a few examples. These would be how to ride a bicycle, how to float in the water, or how to whistle. In all of these cases, you try several times (quite a few for some people), but you do not see any improvement. You really don't know how you did it, but at one point, you found that you could do it. Once you learn how to whistle, float, or ride a bike, you will retain those skills almost all your life even if you do not practice them for many years. Most people can acquire these skills, but a few cannot. There are a couple of examples that everyone acquires. One is how to stand up and walk on two legs, and another is how to acquire a language when you are a child. You were too young to remember how you did these things, but I am sure you have witnessed this with your children. These skills did not come from pure repetition alone. There is a different mechanism in our body that makes them possible. You can experience this if you try to learn a foreign language after you reach adulthood.

Believe it or not, you can find this in some of the karate skills. Most of the techniques are learned through many repetitions. Many senior practitioners may have realized that some things in karate are hard to learn. For instance, *kime* is a technique, and one must learn how to be able not only to tense up but also to relax the body in a certain way to produce a good *kime*.

Here is an excellent sample video of how not to do *kata* practice: http://www.youtube.com/watch?v=Hw3L2mJXagY&sns=fb.

Earlier in this chapter, we observed a video of poor *kumite* performance. The practitioners in both videos were serious, and they genuinely believed what they were doing was good karate. It is very unfortunate that they had unqualified instructors who taught all the wrong practice methods and techniques. Those practitioners learned neither the correct techniques nor how to use them.

The same principle applies to a smaller degree to regular sporting events. It may be easier to understand this point, so let me give you some examples to illustrate it.

Let's take a swimming situation. A swimmer wants to learn how to do the butterfly stroke. As this is a very difficult stroke, let's say he learns it on the ground. After learning the body movements for this stroke, he will eventually be able to simulate all those movements while he is on the ground. This means he learned the technique for this stroke. However, this does not mean he can swim in the water with this stroke even if he knows how to swim using other swimming styles. He needs to get in the water and be able to use this stroke to swim forward. Another example I will pick is a basketball situation. A player learns how to shoot a ball nicely. He learned the technique of throwing a ball. This technique alone does not guarantee that he will have what he needs in a game, which is the ability to make a basket. Making a basket requires other techniques, such as accuracy,

distancing, etc. In baseball, one learns how to swing a bat. Just learning the technique of swinging a bat is not enough, of course. He needs to learn the other requirements, such as timing, distance, etc., so that he can actually hit the ball. However, even that is still not enough. He also has to be able to hit the ball in a way that will make it fly the desired direction and distance. I hope I have made my point regarding this concept.

Now, when you review these cases, you see that this second requirement or technique is much more difficult to acquire than the first one. With the first one, all you need to do is repeat the action. With the second one, you have to acquire a skill that may or may not come with the simple repetition. This is why I say that understanding this point is important for all *karateka*.

So, the ancient masters created *kata* for solo train-ing, but did they expect *kata* to fulfill the particular requirement of learning how to use those base tech-niques? Obviously, they did not. They realized the shortcoming of simply punching the air, so they in-vented the *makiwara*. Hitting a *makiwara* can teach you some things that you cannot learn from practicing *kata* alone. The things you can learn from hitting a *makiwara* include *maai*, accuracy, power delivery, etc. However, the target is fixed, and the distance is the same; therefore, it is lacking in many conditions and situations. For instance, you cannot learn timing as the *makiwara* does not move or react. It also does not teach you *maai* and accuracy in a moving situation as the target is always fixed and immovable. Many modern-day *karateka* use a punching bag as it can move (swing). It is softer, so hitting it feels somewhat similar to hitting a real person. However, the movements of a hanging bag are unfortunately very simple and also predictable. It does not move like a person, so it is still not a perfect training tool.

We can conclude, then, that in order to learn the technique of how to use the base techniques, we need a person or an opponent. You may protest to my conclusion, saying, "What's going on? You told us earlier that *kumite* was not a good training tool for karate training." I am well aware of this, so now I am telling you that the ancient masters taught *bunkai* and not *kumite*. By doing this process, the students learned how to use those base techniques in the *kata*. As you may already know, *bunkai* is an application specific to a technique or a combination. It is not free sparring or anything similar to the free exchange of the techniques in real fighting. You asked earlier why the ancient masters did not create or adopt a *kumite* syllabus in their regular training. There may be two good reasons. One is simply that it was not very feasible because, in those days, a sensei had only one or two students. As I mentioned earlier, the systematic *kihon kumite* became popular only after large-dojo operation came into play in the early twentieth century. Another reason was that they believed that *shiai* (試合, 'competition' or 'tournament') was not appropriate for or suitable to the *bujutsu* concept. This is another interesting and challenging topic, but we will not go into this in this chapter.

We know that this was the belief Funakoshi had, and he did not change his mind throughout his whole life. Nakayama, Chief Instructor of the JKA, had to hold off on the All Japan Championship till 1957, the very year Funakoshi passed. It is true that the Okinawan masters did not officially approve of or teach *jiyu kumite*, but unofficially they did. This is one of the secrets Funakoshi did not share, and the Japanese found out from Choki Motobu (photo right), another Okinawan master who moved to Japan in 1921, that there was an event on Okinawa called *kake dameshi* (掛け試し). Motobu was a very unique karate master. Here is some general information about him from *Wikipedia*: http://en.wikipedia.org/wiki/Motobu_Ch%C5%8Dki.

The word *kake dameshi* is not a popular one in Shotokan karate, so I am happy to introduce it. The first part, *kake*, means 'to throw [a technique]'. The second part, *dameshi*, means 'test' or 'experiment'. But, this word referred to a free fight, almost like a duel (though the purpose was not to kill each other). Supposedly, there were a few open spaces or crossroads in a town where the *karateka* who wanted to test their karate skills would gather at night. Motobu was well known among the karate practitioners as the champion in *kake dameshi*. He was said to be so good that no *karateka* would accept his challenges. So, he used to climb up to the top of a house near the crossing, and he would hide and wait there till an unsuspecting *karateka* passed the area. Then, he would jump down and start fighting without announcing a formal challenge. They say that no *karateka* would dare approach those "dangerous" spots at night anymore. If you are interested in learning more about Choki Motobu, read the article "Through the Myth...To the Man" by Tom Ross at Fighting Arts. There are two parts, and here are the links:

Link 1: http://www.fightingarts.com/content02/motobu1.shtml

Link 2: http://www.fightingarts.com/content02/motobu2.shtml

The ancient masters, with the exception of maybe Motobu, did not openly admit that karate training must include free sparring or street fighting. They claimed it was barbaric and ungentlemanlike. Funakoshi was a highly educated man and a very proud person, so it can be easily guessed that he would definitely forbid such training. And, this was exactly what happened with his teaching in Japan. He was totally against free sparring practice, and his students had to practice *jiyu kumite* secretly. He even resigned from a teaching position at one of the universities when he discovered that his students were secretly practicing free sparring. I will not go into this area of why he did not see the value of free sparring in this chapter. He also prohibited *shiai* throughout his whole life, and I have already mentioned that the first JKA tournament had to

wait till the year he passed. I wonder very much why Funakoshi did not consider or realize the need for the technique of how to use the techniques. This
suspicion is somewhat surprising even to me as Funakoshi was an educator
and was a true believer of *bujutsu* karate.

I will conclude this chapter with the answers to a few of the popular questions about *kata*.

First, let's review what *kata* is again. According to *Wikipedia*, *kata* is a
Japanese word describing "the detailed choreographed patterns of movements
practiced either solo or in pairs." There are many different *kata*, and they rep-
resent samples of fighting sequences. In previous chapters, we have covered
the reasons why the ancient masters created *kata*. The most important message of this chapter is that they did not only create them for the purpose of solo
practice. More importantly, they believed *kata* was the best training tool for
bujutsu karate, the most complex of physical and mental activities.

Hopefully, you agree that our *kata* must be preserved. At the same time,
I am sure you are aware that there are so many unanswered questions with
kata. I listed several of them in the last chapter, and I feel strongly that they
should be answered. If I did this here, however, it would become a much longer book, so, for the purposes of this chapter, I will select the following three
questions and share my thoughts on them. In the future, I may need to write
another book just about the answers to those unanswered questions.

OK, let us start with the first question.

1. Why do *kata* techniques not work in *jiyu kumite*?

Here is a great question that many people wonder about. It is true that
many techniques you practice in *kata* cannot apply or are not usable in your
jiyu kumite. In fact, some people have given up on *kata* because they could not
find an answer that made sense to them. I will attempt to provide the answer
here.

Believe it or not, the answer is quite simple. If you try to apply the *kata* techniques to competition *kumite*, you are figuratively trying to fit a square peg into a round hole. In other words, you are not comparing apples to apples. *Kata* techniques are techniques to maim, hurt, or kill an opponent. You may say that the techniques used in competition *kumite* could hurt or maim the opponent, as well. That is true, but there is one big difference here. The purpose or the objective of the techniques you use in competition *kumite* is to get a point.

If you happen to knock out your opponent or break his bones, you will be disqualified. In addition, there are too many *kata* techniques that are not allowed. For instance, stabbing your finger into the eye, kicking the groin, grabbing the hair, etc., are key techniques in *bujutsu*, but they are prohibited in competition *kumite*. Some of the short-distance techniques, such as *enpi uchi*, knee kicks, *kagi zuki*, and *ura zuki*, are possibly allowed in tournament *kumite*. However, how many times have you seen anyone get a point with one of those techniques? Not too often or never, I suppose.

The reason is obvious and simple. It is extremely difficult to make a visual judgment whether such a technique is effective in a noncontact tournament. A judge needs to see a long-distance technique, such as a straight punch or a kick, to determine if such a technique would be effective. The short-distance movement of an elbow or a knee is much more difficult to judge, so competitors will not try those techniques even if they are allowed.

Then, you may ask, "Do those *kata* techniques work in a real fight?" Of course they do, and that is what you train in with *bunkai*. To be able to use those techniques in a real fighting situation, you must go through the *kata* training cor-

rectly. Let me define the word *correctly* here. Remember the various process-es I have covered in the previous chapters that are needed in learning? You need to learn and acquire the techniques first. Then, you need to do a lot of *bunkai* training to understand how those techniques are used and applied. With *bunkai* training, you need to learn how to use the techniques. There are so many different *bunkai* to each technique, so it is almost impossible to prac-tice and learn all of them. It will take much time, meaning years, to learn one *kata* and its *bunkai*. This is why the ancient masters said you need to spend three to five years on one *kata*.

How do we really know that we are capable of using those dangerous tech-niques? The only way is to test it in a real fight. However, I cannot recommend to anyone to start a bar fight or a street fight just to test this. The samurai of ancient times faced the same dilemma with their sword skill. They either challenged others to a duel or practiced a lot of *kata* and other solo training, such as swinging the sword a thousand times per day. As a real sword was too dangerous to use in daily training with an opponent, they used a *bokken* (木剣, 'wooden sword'), but there were still many serious injuries, including death. So, they came up with another solution in the nineteenth century, which was the invention of the *shinai* (竹刀, 'bamboo sword') and full protectors.

This method became very popular, and you can see this in the modern-day art of kendo. Though *kendoka* may disagree, kendo is no longer *bujutsu* as it lost most of its real kenjutsu techniques. Why and how kendo lost its *bujutsu* parts is an interesting subject, but we will not touch it here.

One thing I want to add here is that the samurai believed *kata* was the best training tool to improve sword fighting skills. The idea of inventing a method using a *shinai* and full protectors was not conceived of all throughout medieval times, when they had many wars and fights. It was invented only at the end of the feudal era of nineteenth century.

2. Can *kata* be changed?

Here is a heavy and also a controversial question.

The ancient masters (as well as the modern-day masters) told us not to change the *kata*; however, many of us know that most, if not all, of the *kata* have been changed to some degree since the time when Funakoshi brought karate to mainland Japan.

In fact, Funakoshi himself changed the *kata*, some slightly (e.g., changing Chinese-sounding names to Japanese-sounding names, switching Heian Shodan and Heian Nidan, etc.) and others greatly (e.g., changing *neko ashi dachi* to *kokutsu dachi*, changing *mae geri* to *yoko keage*, etc.). So, was it OK because he was the master who brought karate to Japan?

Let me share my thoughts and personal opinions on this subject. A wise man once said that there is nothing that does not change except for change itself. I believe *kata* is one of the cultural products that include language, dance, etiquette, customs, etc. No matter how hard we may try to keep these things unchanged, I am afraid it is impossible. *Kata* is no exception. I already mentioned that our Shotokan *kata* have already experienced many changes, and many of these changes came from Funakoshi himself.

Even though I may not be qualified to judge the decision making of Master Funakoshi, after examining the challenging situation in which he was immersed while he was trying to propagate karate in Japan in the early 1920s, I concluded that these changes had to be made and were acceptable changes, if not improvements. I wrote a chapter on this particular subject, and it was included in my recent book, *Shotokan Mysteries* (available from Amazon bookstore). If you are interested in reading further on this subject, I suggest you read my book *Shotokan Mysteries*.

I am not encouraging or supporting, in general, the idea that *kata* can or should be changed. In fact, my stance is that we must keep the *kata* we have exactly the way they are. As *kata* is a textbook and a model, it is a standard

form from which we practice our fighting method. We must have a uniform base from which to learn and teach among the millions of practitioners around the world. All of us forget or remember incorrectly as we practice the *kata* for many years. As the makeup of our individual bodies is different, so we naturally perform the same *kata* differently to some degree. If any of us, whether students or instructors, change the *kata* according to our liking or preference, we will have thousands of different versions. Here is a good example of how *kata* should not be practiced: http://www.youtube.com/watch?v=Hw3L2mJXagY&sns=fb.

So, the conclusion to this question is that only a few masters who truly understand the art of *karatedo* can change the *kata*. The average instructor or practitioner, i.e., almost all of us, must not. Who are those few masters other than Funakoshi? One may be Kanazawa, and another may be Asai (see the next question).

3. Asai Sensei created many new *kata*. Why did he do this?

There are two schools of thought on the number of *kata* one needs to learn. I will not debate which is correct or better. I will only mention a brief description of the two schools. One school's belief is that it is better to concentrate on only a few *kata* and master them thoroughly. This school is headed by Choki Motobu, who was said to have practiced only Tekki (Naihanchi). The real story is that he, of course, knew other *kata* but did not teach very many *kata* in his class. He placed more emphasis on *bunkai* and applications. Apparently, he mainly used techniques from Tekki *kata*, so people incorrectly believed that he knew only one *kata*.

The other school is headed by Master Tetsuhiko Asai (浅井哲彦, 1935–2006), who knew and practiced 150 *kata*. The objective of this school is to learn

many *kata* in order to widen the variety of the techniques. The following statement is very controversial,
but he believed the twenty-six *kata* of the JKA were not
enough to cover all the necessary techniques. He was
the technical director of the JKA for many years during the eighties until the breakup of the JKA in 1990.
After the passing of Masatoshi Nakayama (then Chief
Instructor of the JKA) in 1987, he wanted to change
the JKA syllabus, and this met with very strong opposition from many JKA instructors. After the departure
of Asai in 1990, many of the JKA dojo reduced their *kata* menu to twenty-four
or twenty-five by removing Wankan and/or Jiin from the list.

Of course, it is up to the individual organization to decide how many *kata*
should be practiced. My stance is to keep the number of *kata* small for beginning and intermediate students. Once the practitioner acquires a *dan* rank, I
recommend that he gradually increase the number of *kata* and not stop with
twenty-six *kata* if he is *yondan* or higher. How many more is a difficult question. Altogether, I know fifty or so *kata*. It is extremely difficult to remember
and keep training with all of those *kata*. My memory is poor, so maybe the
younger practitioners would have no problem, but I do not know.

The upside of knowing many *kata* is that it forces you to practice them;
otherwise, you will forget. Another benefit is that you will be able to practice
the additional techniques that are missing in the twenty-six JKA *kata*. However, there are some downsides, too. You will have to spread your time over many
kata; thus, you will have less time to focus on the key *kata* unless you increase
the amount of training time. If you are a Shotokan practitioner, then there are
many instructors who can help you with or teach you the JKA *kata*. There are
only a few who can teach or coach you in the Asai *kata*. If you wish to practice
the *kata* from Shito Ryu or Goju Ryu, then you have to belong to another style
and another dojo. It is possible to learn a *kata* from a video clip, and I have met

many practitioners who do this. I say it is good that they are motivated to learn a new *kata* despite lacking a proper instructor and instruction. I respect that, but, on the other hand, I find that many are practicing incorrect techniques. There are three major problems with this learning method. One is that video is limited in showing the techniques, and viewers can easily misunderstand some of the moves. For instance, sometimes it is not clear if a stance is *sochin dachi* or *zenkutsu dachi*. *Tateken zuki* (vertical punch) can be viewed as *seiken zuki* (regular straight punch).

I find that the more important and possibly serious flaw in learning the Asai-created *kata* by video is that many of the video demonstrations are done by noncertified instructors who learned the *kata* incorrectly. Asai Sensei published a *kata* textbook (in Japanese) for Junro, so for Junro, there is no problem. You can check the textbook and be sure of the techniques. In addition, the video clips of Junro by the JKS are done correctly, and I recommend using them as your training tool. For the other *kata*, we have video in which Asai Sensei himself performs the *kata*, but there are many others for which we do not have his video performance or an official textbook that we can go by. The biggest and most serious problem with video learning is that you will not learn the *bunkai*, which is the heart of the *kata*. Without knowing the true applications from the senior instructors who know the *bunkai*, the *kata* you learned will only be a karate dance.

There are many other interesting questions about *kata*, and most of those questions have not received logical answers. One day I will list those important questions and attempt to provide my thoughts and understanding to shed some light on the mysteries of *kata*.

CHAPTER SIX
第六章

IS WEIGHT TRAINING GOOD OR BAD FOR KARATE?

重量挙げの空手に対する功罪はいかに？

Have you noticed that many Japanese sensei
oppose weight training? Now, I am not referring to the Japanese sensei that live outside
Japan. I am talking about the general consensus of Japanese Shotokan instructors.
As a group, they either oppose or discourage weight training. Though I do not know
what the instructors from other karate styles
would say on this subject, I do know that

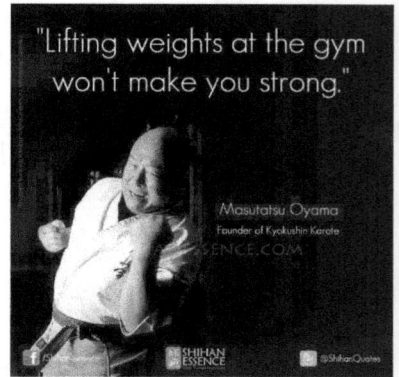

"Lifting weights at the gym won't make you strong."
Masutatsu Oyama
Founder of Kyokushin Karate

many of the Japanese sensei in other *budo*, such as jujutsu, kendo, or even
judo, are not in favor of weight training. One interesting finding is that Mas
Oyama, the founder of Kyokushinkai, left this message: "Lifting weights at the
gym won't make you strong," (photo right). I find this very interesting because
Kyokushinkai is a full-contact style of karate where raw power is needed. In
addition, I know that he himself used to lift weights when he was young. Thus,
you would expect him to encourage the idea of lifting weights to build muscle,
but his message is the exact opposite. He must have changed his view in later
years, or maybe he had a different idea about weight training.

"Power is not necessary."

Here is another quote from the famous
Togakure Ryu Ninjutsu (戸隠流忍術) master,
Hatsumi Masaaki (初見良昭, 1931–). He said,
"Power is not necessary," (photo left). Well, he
is not from karate, but if you watch his training, many of the techniques he uses are very
similar to karate techniques. Apparently, he
does not believe in using power in his techniques. Even though he is old (eighty-three
as of 2014), he can easily subdue opponents who are half his age. Without power, you cannot subdue an opponent, so we wonder why he would say we don't
need power. In this chapter, I hope I can shed light on this subject by sharing

what these instructors believe. You can examine what I present here and be the judge. You can decide at the end if you agree with them or not.

OK, let us start. I realize that this subject is controversial. When I made an announcement on my Facebook page showing the title of this chapter, I received so many comments, both pros and cons. I must also say that it is an important subject and that everyone must have the correct knowledge and understanding about it. I am afraid that many people seem to have some wrong ideas as well as some misunderstanding on some parts of this subject. There are also many good questions, but no senior karate instructors have provided any logical or educated explanations or answers. It is natural that many *karateka* are somewhat confused. I will do my best to provide answers to all the questions I list as well as some explanations that are, hopefully, easy to understand. Let us travel this road together and discover the answers to the different aspects of the important subject of weight training.

First, let us define the term *weight training* and have a clear understanding of what we are discussing. *Wikipedia* defines *weight training* as "[using] the weight force of gravity (in the form of weighted bars, dumbbells or weight stacks) to oppose the force generated by muscle through concentric or eccentric contraction" (http://en.wikipedia.org/wiki/Weight_training).

When we think of weight training, we almost automatically think of lifting heavy barbells and dumbbells. However, weight training also includes using our own body weight (e.g., push-ups, sit-ups, squats, etc.). So, there are two large categories of weight training. One uses some type of weights or equipment, and the other works only with body weight. OK then, let's bring up the questions, and we will see if we can find the answer to each of them.

Do Japanese instructors oppose all weight training?

The short answer is no. This is obvious because they include some type of weight training in their workout, such as squats and sit-ups. Japanese instructors know that all of us need power. Even just to move our body, our muscles have to work. So, they believe making our body strong is the right thing. For instance, if our legs are weak, then we cannot stand in a low stance for a long period of time or shift our body quickly. They particularly believe in the strength of the legs and the midsection, so under a Japanese sensei, you may have gone through some rigorous weight training, such as doing many sit-ups and squats.

Then, why do Japanese instructors say they oppose weight training?

When Japanese instructors, particularly those of the Shotokan style, use the term *weight training*, they are normally referring to weight lifting using either free weights or weight-lifting machines. They normally do not consider exercises using body weight to be weight training. Many of the sensei include sit-ups, push-ups, and squats in their regular karate class. What Japanese instructors have an issue with is lifting heavy weights or power lifting. They may not oppose it completely, but they do discourage it strongly.

Why are they against weight lifting?

The question here is the main issue of this chapter. My explanation will be somewhat long and rather involved. I will do my best to make my explanation simple and clear. I have found that this subject raises a lot of interest among readers and is a controversial one. I am aware that what I write may not sit well with the beliefs of some Western practitioners and instructors.

It is true that weight lifting builds power in your muscles and makes them stronger. Obviously, karate techniques require physical strength, so you wonder what the problem is with gaining power from weight training. Japanese sensei definitely do not consider gaining strength or becoming stronger to be a problem. What is an issue is what kind of weight training is included and how you apply your weight training to the ultimate goal of improving your karate techniques as I assume most readers are *karateka*.

I hope that makes sense so far. Let me elaborate further. First, there is a very important point that we must remember. That point is that there are two separate phases in karate training. One is learning the techniques; the other is delivering or executing them. I have explained this in the previous chapter, "The Reasons Why We Must Preserve Our Kata," so I will not repeat that detailed explanation here. Many instructors know about these phases, but this important fact has not been discussed enough in the past.

In the learning phase, power is not considered to be the most important requirement. In fact, having too much power is considered a handicap or detriment. If you have taught a novice, you probably remember this. Teaching a novice goes like this. You show a simple technique, such as *choku zuki* (straight punch). You tell the novice student to repeat it slowly. What you notice in most students is the overt tension of the arms and shoulders. You see the shoulder on the punching side rise up as it is too tense. We know that the shoulder should be relaxed and pulled down by having the armpit muscles tensed. Students need to be relaxed so that they can perform accurate techniques slowly. Of course, they need minimum power to move their arms and to stand up for a period of time, but they do not need more strength than this during this phase. The other important requirements for karate, such as speed and *kime*, are neither needed nor required at this stage. The most important and challenging thing in this phase is to accurately learn the techniques. At this stage, the sensei will not recommend that the student get involved in weight training except for core muscle training, which will be explained later.

I am sure you will agree with the idea of not focusing on the power aspect when you are just learning the techniques. So, we have no problems up to this point. What we must remember is that many readers are probably either advanced practitioners or instructors. They belong to the next phase, executing the techniques. In their training, they deliver the technique with speed and power. Weight training should increase speed and power. So, why would Japanese instructors oppose it? This is where a more precise explanation is required.

There are at least three apparent reasons why Japanese instructors consider having more power unnecessary and believe that weight training can be harmful even for advanced practitioners.

1. They emphasize the importance of accuracy in karate.

In other words, if your punch cannot land on the target correctly, then a strong punch means nothing. This is the same as a batter in baseball, for example, who can swing a bat with great speed and power. If this batter cannot hit the ball, his fast and strong swing amounts to nothing. This player needs to work on the technique of hitting the baseball. So, for the *karateka*, the ability to execute an accurate technique includes timing, hitting the target, judgment of distance, etc., and is considered more important than sufficient impact (power). Out of all the important requirements (physical side), power is probably considered by instructors to be the least or second least important. Instructors will typically tell you, "You do not need power, but you must have accuracy when you stab the eyes or kick the groin."

2. They consider 5 out of 5 to be better than 5 out of 10.

The aspect of power that Japanese instructors favor heavily is the achievement of its maximum. The numbers I will use here are just for a model of the concept, so the numbers themselves are not important. Here is an example. One person has a maximum power of 5 and can generate all (5) when executing a technique. Another person has a maximum power of 10 but can produce only half (5) because of bad balance, excess tension, etc. Though the final output figures are the same, the first person is better as he is able to maximize body coordination to generate all potential power. The second person wasted half of his capacity, though he tried for the maximum, because of poor balance, excess tension, etc. Of course, if the second person learns how to generate more, then that person will be stronger than the first person. However, the instructors will not recommend that this person work out with weights, but rather that he relax and stretch. By spending his time and effort in this manner, this practitioner can produce more from the existing power capability. Thus, the priority of power is low in Japan, and the sensei will encourage you to work on the other requirements, such as accuracy, balance, rhythm, flexibility, etc.

3. They believe karate techniques to be the most complex of all physical activities.

Though requirements such as speed and power are important, instructors consider technique and skill to be the most important. As I mentioned earlier, no matter how strong or powerful your punch or kick may be, if it misses the target, then such an attacking technique has completely lost its meaning. This is exactly the reason why so many Japanese sensei oppose weight lifting as they believe weight lifting can derail good technique. Let's examine the thoughts behind this.

Before I go into the explanation, let me share my opinion about the free-weight method versus stacked-weight machine method. Both approaches are intended to increase your muscle strength, but if karate practitioners choose to lift weights, I recommend free weights. I know it is easier and safer to train with a weight machine, but you cannot learn the important aspect of balance from a weight machine. This is like trying to learn how to balance on an exercise bike. It is impossible as an exercise bike is fixed to the floor.

When you work with weights, regardless of the methods mentioned above, there are two approaches. One is to lift a very heavy weight, close to the maximum you can lift. In this approach, you can do only a few repetitions. The other approach is to pick a light weight so that you can easily do ten to twenty repetitions. Of course, there are other approaches and combinations of these, but the two approaches I mention here are the typical ones. The first approach is taken mostly by serious weight lifters who wish to either increase the maximum weight they can lift or bulk up (make their muscles bigger). The second approach is chosen mainly by people who are aiming only to tone up their muscles or maintain their strength. For the *karateka* who chooses to lift weights, I hope you are taking the second approach as you do not want to make some of your muscles too strong by using the first approach. Let me explain.

There is nothing wrong with building muscle and gaining strength, but we do not want to just build muscles in karate. There are two main reasons why the sensei oppose the weight-lifting type of training. Here is the first and most important reason. In a later chapter about relaxation, I will list some data about our body parts. For instance, an adult body is made up of 206 individual bones, over 230 movable and semimovable joints (illustration right), and 640 to 850 muscles. Even though the exact numbers of these parts are not important, one thing I want to emphasize is that our body is composed of a huge number of movable parts. They enable us to perform all the complex

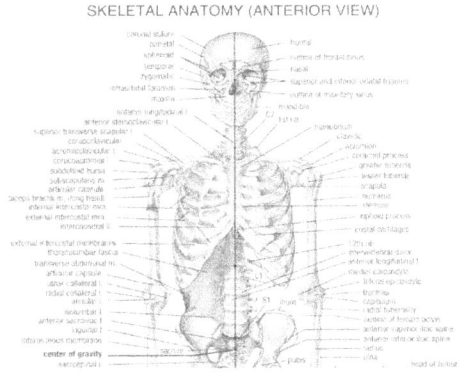

SKELETAL ANATOMY (ANTERIOR VIEW)

movements that are found in karate training. In fact, karate techniques are, believe it or not, some of the most complex movements you can find. Now, remember that we have more than 640 muscles, and they are the power generators. So, imagine our body is like a huge orchestra with more than 800 singers and instruments (640 muscles and 206 bones). Yes, your brain is the conductor who manages them all. You can imagine that it would be a challenging task to make beautiful music, especially if the players and singers are not professionally trained. I am not a musician, so I cannot tell you how challenging it would be, but I am sure it would be quite a challenge for most amateur conductors. What would happen if a certain instrument, such as a drum or a group of drums, started making a much louder sound? Even if you like the sound of the drum, the audience will not be pleased if it is not in harmony with the other instruments. I assume it is pretty easy to understand the importance of harmony and coordination in orchestral music.

Just like orchestral music, when you want to improve karate techniques, what you need most is coordination and harmony. Karate skill is precise work, and numerous amounts of exact repetitions are needed. I am sure you remember, when you were a white belt, how many times you had to repeat *age uke*, *shuto uke*, *gyaku zuki*, *mae geri*, etc., as they were totally new moves for you. Your instructors told you to do those moves slowly but accurately. You did not need power in that process. Refining or improving your techniques is a similar process. It is a work of fine tuning and coordination. Indeed, extra strength is not only unnecessary but is also an unwanted element in that process.

Let me give you another reason why weight lifting is discouraged in karate, and I believe this is a large concern among senior instructors, including me. The action of weight lifting requires contraction and tension. More weight means more tension. I have mentioned several times in the past that karate techniques must be executed with well-balanced and coordinated expansion and contraction. Master Funakoshi also left his message on this in his *Niju Kun*. The nineteenth *kun* states, "*Chikara no kyojaku tai no shinshuku waza no kankyu o wasuruna*" (力の強弱体の伸縮技の緩急を忘るな), meaning 'do not forget the employment or withdrawal of power, the extension or contraction of the body, or the swift or leisurely application of technique'.

Master Taiji Kase (加瀬泰治, 1929–2004), of France, also left a message stating his concern, "Unfortunately, these days I see too much tension in the practitioners' muscles." A practitioner will be off-balance in the harmony of the body mechanism after each weight-training session (tension) unless he makes sure to spend at least an equal amount of time and effort on expanding and stretching his muscles. Most practitioners do not see the ill effects of not doing a counterbalancing exercise until the result gets large enough to see in their performance, at which point it may be too late to reverse the course. Worse yet, practitioners may not see the ill effect at all as they are blinded by the muscle gain and power increase. One may believe he can prove power gain by punching a *makiwara*. It may make a louder sound, but he may not realize that he may now be punching more like a street fighter. How could this be? The bench press is probably the most popular barbell exercise to develop the pectorals (chest muscles). Unless you make an extra effort to keep the elbows inward, they will be kept outward as you do the pressing. I am sure you know what I am talking about if you have bench-pressed before. The body performs exactly how it is taught. It is like a computer. Garbage in, garbage out. We are taught to keep our elbows in as we do the *oi zuki* or *choku zuki*, but the bench press makes a different impression on the chest, shoulder, and arm muscles. The degree of muscle impression and memory is equal to the amount of weight and the number of repetitions.

First of all, why is power or having big muscles more popular in the Western world than in Japan? This is a cultural subject, and my answer may not be accurate or even correct, but I will share my thoughts. At least to me, the need for power and having big muscles seems to be overemphasized in the Western world and possibly underemphasized in Asia, particularly in Japan.

I think it mainly comes from Western machismo. A hero in the Western world often looks like Hulk Hogan, with the huge chest and arms and the small waistline. Consider the case of Arnold Schwarzenegger. When he started in Hollywood, who believed he would become a successful movie star as he could not act or even speak good English? Maybe he learned how to act later, but how was he able to get the job in the first place? I am sure I do not need to tell you the

answer. Builds like that of wrestler Hulk Hogan (photo right) or bodybuilder Arnold Schwarzenegger do not get too much admiration by the majority of Japanese. This is because we consider it artificial and unnatural. We like strong men, too, and that is why sumo is popular in Japan. But sumo wrestlers certainly do not

look like Hulk or Schwarzenegger, though sumo wrestlers are big, too. Many readers may think this sumo wrestler is fat because his belly is sticking out. Believe it or not, the fat content of sumo wrestlers is surprisingly low, being lower than that of the average population. It is true that many of the current sumo wrestlers are fat because they began to believe that having greater body weight could be an advantage. It is true that it is harder to be pushed out of the ring if you are heavy. The Japanese audience does not like this trend, but it is

happening. Compare the way this famous sumo wrestler, Futabayama (双葉山, 1912–1968 [photo right]), looks to the way Hulk Hogan looks. Futabayama had a winning streak of sixty-nine consecutive bouts, a record which has yet to be broken. In fact, though it may sound ridiculous to Western readers, Futabayama would move the organs of his inner belly to shift his balance to his advantage during his matches. I have covered this technique in one of my articles, and I will touch on it again when I mention Rickson Gracie later in this chapter.

Also, what is not widely known about sumo wrestlers is the stretch exercises they must go through. The side split is a requirement for all wrestlers (photo below). Flexibility of the hip joints is considered to be extremely important. With flexible hip joints, a wrestler can do a deep squat, which in turn enables him to push his opponent strongly. However, what is important here is that

they believe flexibility (stretched muscles) will result in more power. This is the biggest difference in the concept of generating more power as the sumo method comes from flexibility, mainly of the hip joints, and not from strengthening the muscles by lifting weights.

Besides having flexible hip joints, it is important to note that they only do the sumo workout in and around the ring. I hear that the younger generation of wrestlers, especially the ones from outside Japan, go to the gym to lift weights. However, most wrestlers still rely on the regular sumo workout to build their power. From this method, they can develop strong but "soft" elastic muscles that are like chewing gum or a rubber tube. The Japanese prefer flexible and soft-looking muscles rather than hard ones that look like rocks. This is the Japanese way of thinking. Maybe you will recall that I wrote an article previously about the Okinawan karate term *muchimi* or *mochimi* (餅身), the 'rice-cake body'. I explained what *muchimi* is and what it does in that article, so you can check it out if you are interested.

I also see a similar difference in the view of power between the swords of the knights and those of the samurai, the katana (刀). The knights' broadswords were built heavy and thick. Their main purpose was to hack at the opponent with the heavy weight of the sword rather than using a sharp cut. It takes, of course, some technique to swing and maneuver the heavy swords, but it definitely requires strong upper-body muscles. On the other hand, katana were tempered to have the finest sharp blade and a slight curve. They were designed and made to slice, cut, and pierce. Of course, a katana is much heavier than a pair of chopsticks but is lighter than a knight's sword. The samurai built their upper-body strength by swinging the swords hundreds of times each day, but they mainly spent their training time in mastering the techniques of using the katana. I am not discussing which sword is better here as each has its own advantages and disadvantages. I am not a hundred percent sure if this difference in swords had any impact or influence on the cultural difference between the modern-day West and Japan. Maybe I am too nostalgic about the knights and the samu-

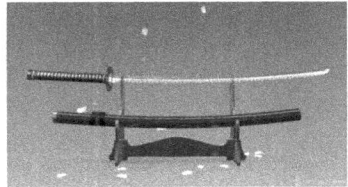

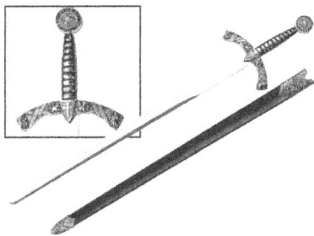

rai; thus, I may be thinking too deeply. However, it would be an interesting study to compare the swords from these two different regions of the world that developed around the same period of history, the fourteenth and fifteenth centuries. Well, it looks as though some people have already done the study. Here is one of the videos, titled *Samurai Sword vs. Knight Broadsword*: https://www.youtube.com/watch?v=EDkoj932YFo.

Now, let's go back to building your power. We have covered that it can be divided into two categories for the purposes of our discussion. One category is lifting weights either to build muscle size or simply to be able to lift heavy weights. In this case, the lifting of the weights does not have a direct connection to sports or the martial arts. In other words, the motion of lifting weights does not simulate the movements of any specific physical activity or skill. This method is suited for bodybuilders and weight-lifting competitors.

The second category is weight training specifically programmed to supplement and enhance the targeted movements of a sport, martial art, or other physical activity.

Let me give you a good example of the other activities that I mentioned in that last sentence. According to *Wikipedia*, "The United States Navy's Sea, Air, Land Teams, commonly known as the Navy SEALs, are the U.S. Navy's principal special operations force." They were highly publicized when a SEAL team attacked and killed Osama bin Laden in 2011, so some readers may remember this. What I want to share is that *Wikipedia* goes on to say that "SEAL training is extremely rigorous, having a reputation as some of the toughest in the world. The dropout rate for SEAL training is sometimes over 90 percent." Take a look at some video clips of a SEAL workout and see how it is done at the following URL (there are three parts to this, so be sure to watch all of them): http://www.youtube.com/watch?v=X4vacQnspQI.

When viewing the workout, you will notice that they either use free weights or they exercise by doing push-ups, lifting logs and boats, or doing hanging exercises that leverage their body weight. These video clips do not cover all

the workouts. I am sure there are a lot more. But, one thing I can almost bet is that they do not use a weight machine to increase power or grow muscles. Their exercises are to develop overall power performance by training mostly on the core muscles rather than the peripheral muscles. If anyone has taken SEAL training, I would like to hear if my assumption is correct. To build the kind of power that can be used in complex actions, this method is obviously preferred, and this is part of the answer to the question we have for karate.

OK, so I brought up SEAL training for one method of building power and endurance, but it does not cover the examples of successful athletes and martial artists. In a later chapter on relaxation, I will pick two Olympic sprinters, Ben Johnson and Carl Lewis. Johnson chose the power approach, and Lewis chose body coordination to increase his speed. I wish to share an interesting fact about another Olympic gold medalist, Michael Phelps, the most decorated Olympian of all time, with a total of twenty-two medals. He did not use any weight lifting in his training (at least up to 2005). Here is an excerpt from the IGN interview in 2005:

> IGN SPORTS: You're 6'4", about 200 pounds. Is your physique all from swimming, or do you hit the weights?
> MICHAEL PHELPS: I've never lifted a single weight in my life. It's all from training in the water, period. That's not to say I wouldn't lift in the future, but now, no.

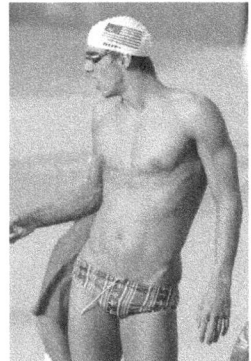

Short-distance swimming is similar to sprinting. Speed is the name of the game, yet Phelps did not choose weight lifting as a method to increase power and speed. Isn't this interesting? Look at how he is built. His body is muscular but rather slender and not bulky at all. Is it only my wild imagination that his build looks like that of a dolphin? It certainly does not look like that of Ben Johnson, a Mack truck, but more like the fluid-looking figures of Carl Lewis or Florence Joyner, who, I believe, relied on natural body-weight training. I believe all these athletes shared the same philosophy and concept as the SEALs on how to train their body to get maximum power and speed. That philosophy is exactly what Japanese martial arts instructors believe and want. Here is the entire IGN interview, which you can read if you are interested in Phelps: http://www.ign.com/articles/2008/08/13/michael-phelps-interview.

OK, the examples I gave above are all sprinters. Now you want to see examples from *budo*. Let me start with a famous person in judo. At the Tokyo Olympics in 1964, when Kaminaga lost in the judo final to Anton Geesink, the Japanese realized for the first time that power could overwhelm technique. Geesink was not only huge (height: 6'6" [1.98 m]; weight: 270 lbs. [122 kg]); he was strong. He basically yanked Kaminaga down and held him for thirty seconds to get an *ippon*. Here is a video clip of his matches at the Olympics: https://www.youtube.com/watch?v=BtyWMKs7dp0.

According to Geesink's book, to develop power, his Japanese sensei, Michigami, made him work with the natural method more than lifting barbells. Michigami told him to run, swim, and bike long distances. He also instructed him to play soccer for leg strength and agility. The photo on the left shows him carrying logs on his shoulders. He would also run up and down the hill to strengthen his legs and upper body. This is interesting as a similar workout with heavy logs is used in SEAL training.

Despite this defeat by a strong Dutch *judoka*, power is still looked down upon not only in the martial arts but also in sports in general in Japan. We have a term used for someone who has an extraordinary amount of strength: *baka chikara* (バカ力), which means 'stupid strength'. Japanese people often wonder why Western people pay so much attention to increasing power or stupid strength. As I have mentioned earlier, it may partially be from the machismo culture in the Western world, e.g., big biceps, chest, etc. People proudly show their half-naked photos on their Facebook pages with their pumped up arms and chest, which the Japanese consider to be a silly act of young people. The other reason is the fact that performance is visible, and the result is much easier to measure in numbers. You can say, "I lifted a hundred kilograms today." On the other hand, it would be much more difficult to see and show your results in numbers for flexibility, balance, timing, etc. People would not be impressed if you said, "Hey, I was able to stand on one leg for five minutes," or, "I was able to touch my toes today."

OK, some may say judo is no longer a martial art. Let me share another example, but this time from MMA. Rickson Gracie, a well-known Brazilian jiu-jitsu fighter who had eleven official matches and retired undefeated in 2000. I was always impressed with his training routine and syllabus. He was known to go to the beach to train on the sand. I do not know if he continues his training now—I hope he does—but he used to practice stretches, relaxation, balancing, and also weight training using his own body (similar to Ginástica Natural). You can find many video clips of his training. Here is the one I like the most: http://www.youtube.com/watch?v=tTi_E78DSK4.

He is also known to practice yoga, especially with the breathing methods that exercise his abdominal muscles. In the training video, I believe you can see how he moves his belly up and down. In fact, this exercise made him capable of moving and shifting his internal organs. Believe it or not, he can

change his center of gravity by doing this. This may not sound like a significant fact, but this is, in fact, why he was so difficult to dislodge once he got on top of his opponent. There are many videotapes of his fights, so you can see

this. His winning did not come from hitting or kicking from a standing position as he is a Brazilian jiu-jitsu practitioner. He used to take his opponent down to the floor then straddle him and beat him until the helpless opponent gave up. You may wonder why a well-trained and strong opponent would not be able to dislodge him from that position. Well, the special ability of Rickson was that he could shift his internal organs to keep perfect balance. Lifting weights was never a part of his routine or workout program. He believed in his method, and it certainly paid off in his fights. He was undefeated in MMA for many years, which proves his ability and skill. At the same time, he also proved that his method worked.

If I investigated and researched more, I am sure I could come up with more examples of who has followed or is following this type of workout, but I believe I have given enough examples. So, next let us discuss why they chose to take this method, which is more natural yet more creative in many ways than just lifting weights.

My assumption is that these athletes and performers knew, maybe instinctively, that what it takes is total performance, which requires a lot of harmony and coordination within their body. In other words, what total performance meant for them was not the simple sum of the power in different parts of the body. Having stronger arms or legs is good only if they are in perfect tune and coordination with the rest of the body. If one lifts heavy weights, it probably takes two or three times the training to put those arms and legs back into harmony and coordination. Given the amount of effort necessary for this process, they figured out that it is more effective and wise to train using the holistic core-training approach rather than the partial approach.

There is one thing I must share with the reader. I find that there is a serious ignorance and underappreciation among us, including karate practitioners, regarding what our body does and how it does it. I know this is a strong statement, and it may offend some people. I want to emphasize that I am not using the word *ignorance* to demean practitioners. Rather, I want to catch their attention so that they will realize what they are missing or are having little respect or appreciation for. Thus, I decided to include this in this chapter as I consider this subject to be critically important in order for us to

understand what we have been discussing up to this point. I get very upset when I see an instructor who allows or orders white belts or kids to do *jiyu kumite* (free sparring). The instructor would say, "Yes, white belts (or kids) are terrible, but this will teach them to have fighting spirit." The instructor may have done this with good intentions, but, sadly, he does not realize how much damage he has done to this white belt (or child) in his learning of the karate techniques. If you want to teach fighting spirit, then you must wait till the student learns the fighting techniques first. You may wonder why I oppose *jiyu kumite* for children. It is not because it can be dangerous. As it would take a lot of space, I will not include the explanation in this chapter. I will find another opportunity one day to explain why kids should not be doing *jiyu kumite*, which is probably another big controversial subject.

I am not blaming only karate practitioners and instructors. I am afraid this is a general trend in the field of athletics, including, believe it or not, professional-level athletes. In fact, the complexity of the body mechanism is not appreciated or respected enough by most of the general public. I make a similar statement in another chapter, "Why Is Relaxing Our Muscles So Difficult?" I mentioned the topic of taking for granted our ability to walk with ease, though the mechanism of standing and walking is extremely complex and difficult. So far, no mechanical robot has been able to imitate the walking movements of a person precisely. But, we do it so easily that we do not appreciate our ability every time we walk. You would discover an appreciation for this ability if you were to lose it, say, from an accident or a stroke. You would experience extreme difficulty if you had to relearn how to walk through rehabilitation. It might take months or even years to regain the ability to walk, which you never would have dreamed of. Read the article "Walking After a Stroke" from HealthDay to understand what happens when you encounter a stroke. Anyone can have a stroke, no matter your age, race, or gender, so it could happen to any of us. The patient in the article was only fifty-two years old. See the article at this link: http://consumer.healthday.com/encyclopedia/high-blood-pressure-24/blood-pressure-news-70/walking-after-a-stroke-part-1-645712.html.

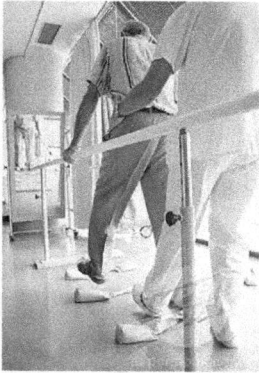

Now you understand that walking is a complex body mechanism, but it takes many muscles and a lot of body coordination to carry out even a simple action like picking up a glass. It may be surprising to many readers, but a movement like picking up a glass with your hand is mechanically difficult as it is a fine, complex movement that requires very precise and harmonized neurophysiological coordination, such as detecting the hardness and weight of the glass. A fine and precise balancing act is required even though we may not recognize it as we can do this action almost unconsciously. Have you ever tried to pick up something light that looked very heavy, such as a glass filled with water? I am sure you ended up spilling the water as you picked it up too fast, believing it was very heavy. Indeed, even just to pick up a glass of water requires the perfect coordination of many muscles, not only in your hand and arm, but also in your upper body. Not only that, it also simultaneously requires visual coordination with the neural processes in the brain and spinal cord, which control, plan, and relay motor commands. Here is a paragraph from "The Anatomy of Movement" by Susan Schwerin, PhD, at Brain Connection (http://brainconnection.brainhq.com).

> ...[T]o pick up a glass of water can be a complex motor task to study. Not only does your brain have to figure out which muscles to contract and in which order to steer your hand to the glass, it also has to estimate the force needed to pick up the glass. Other factors, like how much water is in the glass and what material the glass is made from, also influence the brain's calculations.

If you still believe picking up a glass is easy, how about handling a pair of chopsticks? Can you pick up a small round bean or something very soft like tofu? Yes, it takes a lot of training, but you can learn to do it. Do you not agree that we really must appreciate and respect more of what our body does and can do for us?

To understand our motor coordination more, you can read the basic concepts that are explained in the *Wikipedia* article on this subject: http://en.wikipedia.org/wiki/Motor_coordination.

Now I need to bring up another important fact. It is that the body is designed to do what it has learned or repeated many times. I am sure you will agree with this concept that we normally do what we have repeated or practiced most. Some may say, "Yes, this is why we are supposed to do our *kata* many times." Tsutomu Ohshima (大島劼, 1930–) said we have to repeat *kata* 150,000 times before we can think the *kata* is ours. I am not sure if that number is really appropriate, but he was right about the necessity of repetition to learn and understand only one *kata*. If you have trained under any of the Japanese sensei, I am sure you have found that they like repetition.

OK, I need to bring up one more important concept that you are probably already very familiar with. You know that it is difficult to kick an old habit. When you were a novice, did your sensei tell you to rub your elbow against the side of your body when you did a *choku zuki*? Our natural body movement for punching is to bring the elbow out like a round punch. Punching straight like a *choku zuki* is a new technique for a novice, and I am sure it was difficult

for you to change your arm movement to something different from that of a street-fighting style (photo right). This is why you want to learn a technique correctly FIRST. It is possible to change later, but it will take much time and effort to change or make an adjustment to the technique as it was learned initially.

You may ask how this is related to the subject of weight lifting and karate training. If you think a little more, it is not a difficult question to answer. We have talked about the fact that our body will do the movements that were learned (repeated). You must remember that lifting weights leaves a big impression on muscle tissue with movements that are dissimilar to karate movements. You will teach your muscles to move in the way you lift weights. Because of the weight, the muscle memory will be several times stronger than it would have been if those same movements had been done without any weight.

Then, remember how complicated the body movements that your karate techniques require are. Those movements demand that a lot of muscle groups harmonize and coordinate in ways that are totally different from the movements you do when lifting weights. Thus, most strengthening of the peripheral muscles, such as the biceps and the pectorals, has very little positive effect on karate techniques. In fact, it could turn out to be a hindrance to the coordination and harmonization of the muscle groups that are required for karate techniques.

Some may wonder if karate movements and techniques are really that complicated. After practicing karate for many years, many readers may feel almost natural when doing a *kata* or a series of *kihon* techniques. But, seriously, karate techniques are indeed extremely complicated. This very point is undermined or taken for granted by many practitioners and athletes. I consider karate and martial arts techniques to be the most difficult of all physical activities. I am not talking about only the techniques per se. I am aware that some of the techniques in ballet and gymnastics are physically more demanding and difficult. However, the requirements of the martial arts demand both conscious and unconscious reactions. I have already explained this in detail in the previous chapter, "The Reasons Why We Must Preserve Our Kata". So, I will not repeat the explanation, but the basic concept that differs (and puts the martial arts in the highest category) is the concept of not having any rules, meaning that there is no attacking or defending side nor are there any dos or don'ts.

This is why an extremely high level of reaction and reflex ability is required in karate. One may be able to execute a technique in a conscious state (during training or in the dojo), but he may not be able to do so in an unconscious state (in a real fight or in a dark alley), which is the stage where the techniques must come out without being thought about. Bruce Lee said, "Don't think. Feel!" He was right, and that is the ultimate stage we need to reach in the martial arts. But, to get to that ultimate stage, we must first be able to perfect the techniques in our

conscious state, training. Therefore, unnecessary weight lifting can be a monkey wrench thrown into the precise machine that is our body. The unfortunate thing is that weight training is often done with good intentions and without a real understanding of the negative side.

Let me give you one very interesting case. I read a story about one of the professional golfers. I forget his name, but he became well known in professional golf circles about twenty years or so ago. He was a young and up-and-coming champion at that time. He wanted to drive the ball farther, of course. So, to increase his power, he decided to go up to Alaska and become a lumberjack for a significant amount of time. He certainly believed it would help. He would swing a very heavy ax to chop at trees in a manner similar to swinging a golf club. I do not remember exactly how many months or years he stayed there and chopped trees, but it was not a few days or even weeks. He returned to the golf circuit and discovered the shocking reality. His golf form was totally destroyed, and he could no longer play the game at a professional level. I remember that he was never able to regain his form, and he eventually disappeared from the circuit. If any of the readers happen to know who this player was, please let me know. I want to find out what became of him.

How beneficial are those training tubes we use in our dojo?

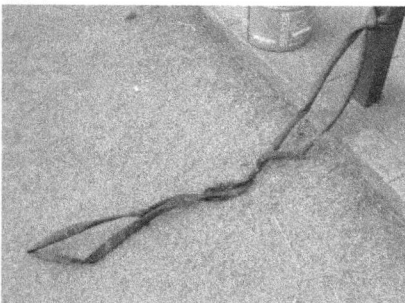

Old bicycle tire tubes are a popular training tool in many Shotokan dojo. I used to use them a lot during my younger days and have fond memories of hard training using those tubes. A short answer is that any exercise is good if done correctly. I used to believe the tube had to be fully extended and you had to fight it out by pushing or pulling it to its limit in order to get the best benefit. Recent research has proven that my understanding was wrong.

The fact that the tube will give you the least resistance at first and the most when it is fully extended will not result in the best performance for karate. In other words, you may gain some power in your arms or legs, but the speed of your punch or kick will not improve. In fact, it was discovered that extensive training with the tube is not good for your elbows and knees. What you need, instead, is a machine or a tool that gives you the most resistance at first then gives you less as you proceed with your punch or kick. Unfortunately, at this time, we do not have such a machine or tool that would provide that kind of training condition. This is why I dropped the tube training from my workout menu as well as from the classes I teach. One alternative is to find a partner who can give you that condition by pulling strongly against your moves at the initial stage then letting go gradually. Well, anything is possible.

How about the use of the weight jacket/vest?

When I was training full time, I used to use a vest like this (photo right). If your body weight is in line with the healthy weight chart, then you could wear one of these. This will work on your foundation and help you strengthen your legs. One thing you must remember is that it has a minor ill effect on your form as your body is now artificially heavier. If you pay much at-

Weight Vest 20kg
パワーベスト20Kg
Produced by JTW

tention to keeping your posture correct, then there will not be much negative effect. I suggest putting weight bars in the lower pockets around the waist and keeping the chest area free so that you will not have the obstacles that would limit your arm movements. If you are overweight, then you do not need an extra vest. What you need to do first is to reduce your body weight to a healthy level before you consider wearing a weight jacket or vest.

Aren't jogging and cardio exercise beneficial?

As I stated earlier, any moderate exercise is good for your health. But, if this is to supplement your karate training, I say, "Why would you spend time jogging or on an exercise bike if you can do your *kata* or stretches at home?" You can get a lot of cardio-oriented exercise if you do *kata* nonstop for fifteen or thirty minutes. That would be a lot more beneficial to your karate improvement, and you wouldn't have to drive to the gym.

If your excuse is that you don't have a big enough room to do *kata*, you can always go to the park. If you are embarrassed doing it in front of people, go to the park at 4:00 or 5:00 AM. Then you will find very few people. This is how the tai chi people train normally. It is simply a matter of desire. Most of the reasons I hear are, I hate to say, only excuses.

Is there anything wrong with going to the gym to do exercises?

Once again, there is nothing wrong with doing exercises, whether you do them at home or at the gym. Some say they need an environment to exercise, and their homes are not suitable. Others say they need some exercise equipment. Regardless, I just do not understand why they do not spend that time on karate training. It may be a supplemental workout to the karate training, but I am afraid they will get tired from the workout at the gym and skip or downgrade the karate training. One thing we must remember is that we need to spend the same amount of time or more on karate (precision work) to compensate for the muscle workout (nonprecision work or nonkarate movements). So, I hope you can plan plenty of time for your karate training if you are going to engage in supplemental workouts.

I must mention that weight-training tools are commonly used by the Okinawan styles. They use many different tools, some of which are heavy, such as *chiishi* (チーシ [#1]), *sashi* (サーシ [#2]), *kame* (カメ [#3]), etc. What benefits do the Okinawan styles expect from working with these weight tools? Are they beneficial for Shotokan practitioners?

1   2   3

First, these exercises are called *hojo undo* (補助運動, 'auxiliary exercises'), which are designed to support or supplement the karate techniques. This is a part of the regular dojo training syllabus at an Okinawan-style dojo. In most Shotokan dojo, we do not train with these tools, but it is an important part of Okinawan karate training.

My understanding of these tools is that they are for strengthening the joints, especially the wrists and shoulders, as well as the arm and finger muscles. Wrist (twisting) power is necessary in close-range fighting. We see many *maki* (巻き, 'twisting') or *kaiten* (回転, 'turning') techniques in many of our *kata*, such as Bassai, Hangetsu, Kanku, etc. For Shotokan, a typical *bunkai* for these techniques is to block the punches. In that case, great twisting or grabbing power is not needed; however, as you know, there are many different *bunkai*. It could be that the opponent grabbed your clothes or your wrist. In that case, you would need much more wrist-twisting strength. You can develop twisting strength by swinging a *chiishi* (#1 above). With a *sashi* (#2 above), you punch slowly. The immediate purpose is to refine the course of your punch so that it will travel straight with the connection with your *hara*. After accomplishing this, your punch will become faster and more powerful. This may be confusing, but I must emphasize that this exercise is not designed to have the direct result of building power and speed by strengthening the muscles with the *sashi*.

The *kame* (#3 on the previous page) is used for strengthening gripping power, and this is definitely for the purpose of fighting at a short distance. At the same time, the weight of the vases will work on the shoulder muscles and the foundation (legs and stance). I would like to hear from the practitioners of Okinawan karate whether my understanding is correct or if I have missed something.

Finally, let's discuss what core-muscle training is.

First, we need to know what the core muscles are. In short, they are the muscles around your trunk and pelvis, typically located beneath the surface muscles. According to *Wikipedia*,

> in anatomy, the core refers, in its most general of definitions, to the body minus the legs and arms. Functional movements are highly dependent on the core, and lack of core development can result in a predisposition to injury. The major muscles of the core reside in the area of the belly and the mid and lower back (not the shoulders), and peripherally include the hips, the shoulders and the neck. (*http://en.wikipedia. org/wiki/Core_(anatomy)*)

The core muscles are also called the *inner muscles* as many of the muscles are hidden beneath the exterior musculature that people typically train. The deeper muscles include the transverse abdominals, multifidus, diaphragm, pelvic floor, and many other deeper muscles. What we consider to be the most important core muscles are those that connect the pelvis to the legs (mainly the area between the knee and the thighs). Believe it or not, there are many muscles there, but the main ones are the psoas major, the

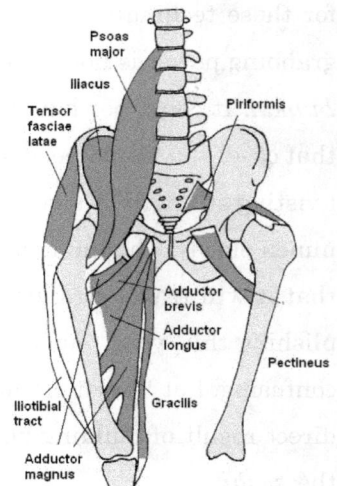

iliacus, the sartorius, the pectineus, the adductor longus, the adductor brevis, the adductor magnus, the biceps femoris, the semitendinosus, and the semi-membranosus, among others.

Why are these muscles important?

Your core most often acts as a stabilizer and force transfer center rather than as a prime mover, and this is why the core is important for karate. We must consider core strength as the ability to produce force with respect to core stability, which is the ability to control the force we produce. One other important benefit of exercising the core, research has shown, is that athletes with higher core stability have a lower risk of injury. According to a Mayo Clinic article, core exercises improve your balance and stability.

> Core exercises train the muscles in your pelvis, lower back, hips and abdomen to work in harmony. This leads to better balance and stability, whether on the playing field or in daily activities. In fact, most sports and other physical activities depend on stable core muscles.

Interestingly, it also states that core exercises don't require specialized equipment or a gym membership. For more on this subject, read http://www.mayoclinic.org/healthy-living/fitness/in-depth/core-exercises/art-20044751?pg=1.

Obviously, the hip area is the most important part of your body when we talk about body movements. Most people understand that the legs are important when you walk, run, or simply shift your body. Many may believe these movements are done solely by the muscles in the legs, but that is not the case. Unfortunately, not too many karate practitioners truly under-

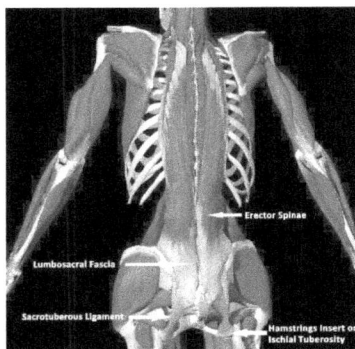

stand that such movements must accompany the highly sophisticated coordination of various muscle groups as well as the heavy involvement of the muscles that are located near the pelvis or lower abdominal area (see illustration on the previous page). In addition, even fewer people know or appreciate that the coordination and the harmony of these core muscles have a great impact on all other bodily motions, especially the ones that require precision work or sophisticated skills. The work of these inner muscles in precise harmony and coordination can result in extraordinary power generation as well as exceptional technical skills. For instance, you need this ability if you wish to do a one-inch punch. This ability is exactly what is needed if a serious karate practitioner wishes to obtain such ability and skills.

Modern medical science is only recently proving this fact, which was known hundreds of years ago by the samurai, who had no medical knowledge. They knew this from their physical experience after training intensively for many hours every day. When one pushes his body to its ultimate level with severe training, he begins to develop internal eyes (self-awareness), which reveal the functions of the internal body. This may sound like mysticism, but it is not. I am simply touching on an area of unknown human capability that will eventually be proven by modern science, though it is not at this time. This experience was recorded by Egami, and if you are interested, you can read his book, *The Heart of Karate-Do*.

You may say, "OK, I understand that the inner muscles in the hip area are important, but how about the big muscles like the pectorals and the belly muscles? Aren't those six-packs in the belly, rectus abdominis, a part of the core muscles?" All of the muscles in our body are important in general. However, we do not consider those muscles that are located on the surface of our body to be core muscles. The core muscles are located internally or in a deeper part of our body. The other important muscle for body movement, in addition to the muscles of the pelvis area, is the erector spinae (the major back muscles, illustration right). Though they are not directly connected to the legs, they are eventually connected to the hamstrings, and they play an important role in the movement of the body. They are the main supporter of the upper body. They work in balance with the internal and external abdominal oblique muscles as well as with rectus abodminis to keep our balance while we stand and to give mobility to the body.

I must review that there are two types of weight exercises to strengthen your muscles. One type is done for moving techniques, and the other type is for foundation building. Let me give you an example. Doing punches with a *sashi* or a tube is the first type. In this case, you need to follow up with the same technique without the weight, spending twice as much time and effort on the follow-up exercise. This is because your focus when punching with the weight is not typically on the accuracy or speed of the technique. You need to do a follow-up exercise without the weight so that you can repeat the technique while paying close attention to accuracy with speed in order to gain the benefit in the targeted technique. This type of exercise is not considered to be core muscle training.

Exercises such as deep squats and leg raises are to strengthen your core muscles. The purpose of these exercises is not to imitate the karate techniques but to strengthen the stance, the foundation of the body. These exercises should be included in your training menu but should be done separately from the karate training. You do not want your core muscles to be tired before karate training. Your attention to learning and repeating the karate techniques will be reduced if your core muscles are already tired. You want to maintain a hundred percent of your attention on the techniques during

karate training. There are many other core exercises, but I will not go into the specifics here. I have already given some hints as to where to look for the information, so I ask the reader to do his own research and investigation to learn how to exercise these important muscles.

One more concept that I must share, which is a deeply embedded concept among the Japanese with regard to the martial arts, is *shin gi ittai* (心技一体), which literally means 'mind and technique are one'. This means that the mind and the body must harmonize and work together. We have been discussing how to strengthen our body, but we did not touch on the mental aspect. Why? Because most of us think only of physical techniques when we think of karate. This is one of the concerns I have with many practitioners. And, this is why I wanted to bring this up at the end of this chapter. Remember one of the precepts of Funakoshi's *Niju Kun*? He wrote in the fifth *kun*, "*Gijutsu yori shinjutsu*" (技術より心術), meaning 'mentality over technique'. He told us that mental technique is more important than physical technique. He, I am sure, believed both were equally important, but he had to say this because most of us tend to forget about the mental aspect of *budo* and karate. How do we strengthen our mental technique? We certainly cannot do so by lifting weights.

A skillful *karateka* without honor and respect is only a hoodlum. A *karateka* who is strong but who has a chicken heart will not be able to defend himself or his family when a life-or-death situation arises. The Japanese sensei know this, but we find it difficult to teach this. Let me quote the words of Takayuki Mikami (三上孝之, 1933– [photo right]). He said, "The hardest thing to teach in karate is *budo* spirit, but it is the most important aspect the art of karate can offer to its practitioners."

Many experts tell us that the greatest enemy is ourself. How do we win against ourself? How do we overcome fear and ego? Are there any training methods to strengthen our mind? As this chapter is not on this subject, I will not spend much time on this, but I will share this with the reader. The hints can be found in the *Niju Kun* and the *Dojo Kun* (道場訓).

Conclusion

We have agreed that power is necessary for every one of us to move and do any physical activity. We have also agreed that the stronger a technique is, the better it is. However, we have also found that excessive weight lifting without a well-planned strategy is unwise and not recommended as such activities can be harmful and possibly detrimental to our karate techniques. We have discovered that our body, despite looking simple, is really a very delicate and complex mechanism that requires a tremendous amount of fine tuning and organized training to carry out even a simple movement.

Another important discovery is that karate techniques (and those of the martial arts in general) are the most difficult and complex physical activity compared to any other sport or art when we examine the physical and mental structure. We also learned that even a simple movement requires a group of muscles to function. This means that any one of the karate techniques requires the total coordination of various muscle groups so that the muscles will perform in harmony. Strengthening a certain muscle or muscle group can be a monkey wrench, such as an electric guitar in a classical music orchestra (with all due respect to electric guitar players). This is the primary reason why Japanese sensei are against weight lifting.

Most importantly, we found that lifting weights to strengthen the peripheral muscles, such as the biceps and the pectorals, has much less value compared to the strengthening of the core muscles. Those muscles are typically called the *inner muscles* and are hidden beneath the exterior musculature, most of them being found in the lower abdominal area. Your core most often acts as a stabilizer and force transfer center. Also, core strength is the ability to produce force with respect to core stability, which is the ability to control the force we produce. Mayo Clinic reports that core exercises improve your balance and stability. In fact, most sports and other physical activities depend on stable core muscles. Though Japanese instructors dislike weight-lifting exercises, they include exercises that strengthen the core muscles in the hip and lower-back areas.

Our legs are the foundation as well as the transportation tool; thus, they need to be strong and movable. This is not only true for runners but also for karate practitioners. The leg bones are connected to the pelvis and supported by many inner muscles. Those inner muscles are more difficult to train and strengthen than those that are visible. Most of the visible muscles easily become weak without consistent training. On the other hand, the core muscles remain strong for a much longer period. Due to the peculiarity of the location, the core or inner muscles are easier to train using our own body weight rather than using weight-lifting tools. Research has shown that athletes with higher core stability and strength have a lower risk of injury. In an interview conducted by *Shotokan Karate Magazine* in 1994, Tetsuhiko Asai (浅井 哲彦, 1935–2006) said, "*Karateka* must aim to control every part of their body as a unit and separately. Relaxed, strong and flexible muscles are the key." He was telling us that strong muscles are important, but, at the same time, they must be relaxed and flexible. We must spend our training time not only in strengthening the muscles but also in stretching and breathing deeply so we can be relaxed and flexible. In Asai karate, we list three key elements we need to prepare before practicing karate. They are flexibility, balance, and strength. We also need to look at the strength of our mind as we strengthen our body to perfect our karate. To achieve the ultimate height of *karatedo*, one must have both a strong

body and a strong mind. So, when we spend time strengthening our body, we must also plan to spend an equal amount of time strengthening our mind.

Do you think you were doing your weight training correctly, and was it beneficial to your karate techniques? Did you consider the facts described in this chapter in your weight training? As I believe you are a serious *karateka*, maybe you will want to consider these facts when you do your weight training next time. I am sure you want to see the time and effort you put in result in improvement of your karate, do you not?

CHAPTER SEVEN
第七章

WHAT IS KI?
気とは何ぞや？

This is a deep and complex subject. There are a large number of books written in Japanese on this subject, ki, but unfortunately, articles and books in English and other languages (other than Chinese) are rare. I have thought about writing on this subject for a long time but have always hesitated as it is so involved. I plan to write a longer and more comprehensive piece in the future, but for this chapter, I will cover mainly the part that is related to karate and its relationship to breathing.

合気道 十段 引土道雄書 氣

OK, let us start. For many readers, ki may be a mysterious and possibly dubious Asian concept, but it really is not, and I wish to shed some light on the subject. In essence, ki is the source or the energy that gives life. In other words, it is something that is enabling us to live. As long as you are alive, you have ki in you as a living being. When you die, your ki is believed to return to nature. All living things, such as animals, insects, and plants, have their own ki. In fact, we Japanese believe that even nonliving matter and objects in nature, such as stones, mountains, lakes, rivers, rain, lightning, clouds, stars, etc., have their own ki in them. This is why we have feng shui (風水), a Chinese system of geomancy believed to use the laws of both Heaven (Chinese astronomy) and Earth to help one improve life by receiving positive qi or chi. The term *feng shui* literally translates as 'wind water' in English. If you are interested in this art, you can look it up on *Wikipedia*, which explains its history and theories. The basic concept is that different natural factors, such as directions, mountains, rivers, etc., have different energies. Different combinations have a positive or negative impact on people. Asians, particularly the Chinese, take this very seriously, and feng shui becomes one of the major deciding factors when they choose a house. This is very popular even with the Chinese people living in the U.S. and probably in Europe, too.

Anyway, we believe everything has its own energy and its own unique vibration (*hado* [波動]) called *ki* (気). This is a profound concept as modern physics (special and general relativity) came to realize only a century ago that everything in the universe consists of energy and that the base construction is vibrations (waves) created by energy. Even if you do not know quantum physics, you know Einstein's famous energy formula, $E=mc^2$, which he announced in 1905. Mass-energy equivalence is the concept that the mass of a body is a measure of its energy content. In this concept, mass is a property of all energy, energy is a property of all mass, and the two properties are connected by a constant. So, the 3,000-year-old Chinese concept cannot be considered totally groundless or unbelievable.

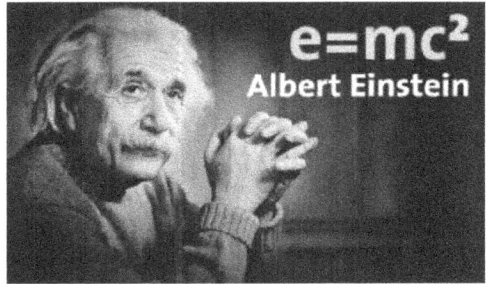

Though the concept of ki extends to everything in the universe, let us look at only the ki that is related to us, the people here in this chapter.

When we look at our body, we find different waves and patterns. The most obvious one that we all know of is our brain waves. Another one is blood pressure, which changes in general patterns throughout the day. There are other not-so-visible or not-so-noticeable physical conditions, such as body temperature and hormone level, which also fluctuate during the day.

A circadian rhythm is something you will notice only when you travel a long distance, covering different time zones. According to *Wikipedia*, "a circadian rhythm is any biological process that displays an endogenous, entrainable oscillation of about 24 hours. These 24-hour rhythms are driven by a circadian clock, and they have been widely observed in plants, animals, fungi, and cyanobacteria." One's hormone level changes by the hour and is tied to a circadian rhythm, so you may need help from melatonin tablets to be able to sleep during your overseas trips. Most of these cycles and waves are closely tied to the tides and the changing of night and day.

So, ki is the energy source in our body that can affect the waves and cycles of our bodily functions. If everyone has this ki, then how do we increase it? In fact, there are two ways to increase the energy in your body. One is what everyone does every day, eating and drinking. This is an external source. This is why your diet is important to your health. The other source is internal, and it is ki, which was discovered or recognized a few thousand years ago in China. In the Western world, ki was not discovered or recognized. Instead, the area of the mind was developed by modern-day psychologists, notably by Sigmund Freud (1856–1939) and Carl Jung (1875–1961 [photo left]). This came about only around the mid-nineteenth century. If you have consistent depression, your doctor will tell you that you are having some chemical malfunction in your head, so he recommends that you take some medication (an upper) to raise your spirits. On the other hand, a ki master or ki doctor will tell you that your ki is weak and point out specific areas of your body that are lacking in ki or where the ki flow is slow or blocked. He may suggest acupuncture or moxa treatment along with breathing exercises. These treatments will stimulate the local ki, which results in better flow of ki throughout your body. The ki doctor may also give you some medication that is not made of chemicals but mainly of herbs and natural ingredients. It is taken in the form of tea or soup.

The difference in treatments and diagnoses between the two schools does not stop with the mental aspect. It also gets into the physical domain. When you have back pain, or if you suffer from some type of allergy, you can resort to acupuncture, moxibustion, or herbal treatments. Acupuncture (*hari* [鍼]) is famous even in the Western world. Moxibustion or moxa cautery (*kyu* [灸]),

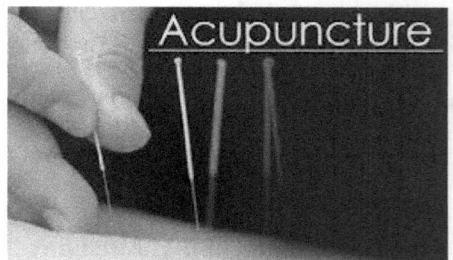

which is shown in the photo to the right, is
probably not as well known, but it is a very
popular medical treatment for many illness-
es in Asia. I remember that my grandmother
used to put a lot of pieces of moxa on her
shoulders and back to ease her headaches,
backaches, and arthritis pains. In case you do not know about moxibustion,
it is where you ignite what looks like a piece of an incense stick. It burns very
slowly and, in fact, burns your skin as a stimulus that gives a shock or boost
of energy to the ki spot that needed the energy (ki). I have tried it, so I know
it burns. I have also tried acupuncture, and I like that more than moxibustion. Anyway, there are more radical medical treatments using ki. One is ki
anesthesia, and the other is ki operation. You might have seen video clips on
these treatments. They are all related to ki and its flow. I will not go into these
particular treatments as I do not have any experience in them, and my focus in
this chapter is not the medical applications of ki. There are some extraordinary
reports of such treatments, so you can look for the video clips and other reports
if you are interested.

I give a lot of credit to modern Western medicine and medical accomplish-
ments, so I am not discounting or bad-mouthing those treatments. To find a
cancer symptom, you must go to a hospital and have an X-ray taken. However,
in the areas of prevention, light illness, and especially the early stages of illness, I believe natural treatments and ki training may be a better choice and
would make more sense. I want to emphasize that I am not a medical doctor, so
I am not qualified to give medical advice or recommendations.

We believe that our body system is run by or filled with waves and cycles.
When they are out of tune or imbalanced, we get in a situation or condition
called *sickness* or *illness* (both physical and mental). So, the ancient people created various ways to strengthen the ki and maintain the patterns steady and
balanced. These methods include *chi gong* or *kiko* (気功), yoga, Zen meditation

(*zazen* [座禅]), and *tai chi chuan* or *tàijíquán* (太極拳) along with some kung fu (功夫) styles and a few other martial arts, such as aikido (合気道).

I practiced Nishino-style *kiko* (Nishi-no Ryu Kiko Ho [西野流気功法]) in Tokyo for three years (1998–2000). I included the experiences I had at Nishino Dojo in my recent book, *Shotokan Mysteries*, so I will not repeat them here. I will only say that the training was mainly to relax your muscles with deep-breathing exercises. Let me point out that tai chi can be an excellent ki-building system but only when it is taught correctly with its breathing method. It is an internal martial art practiced for both its defensive training and its health benefits, but moving slowly alone will not ensure ki building. It must be done with a proper breathing exercise in a way that is harmonious with the body movements. In fact, for ki building alone, tai chi is a better method than karate training. I will explain why I say this later.

Chi gong, yoga, Zen meditation, and *tai chi chuan* are, in essence, the slow-moving exercises that are closely tied to deep breathing. You may wonder why I include Zen meditation in ki building. I can see why you would wonder this as there are no body actions in Zen meditation. There may seem to be no movements as the arms and legs are still. However, Zen meditation, if done with deep breathing, requires a lot of movement in your lungs, diaphragm, and abdominal and inner muscles. By breathing deeply, you will strengthen the diaphragm and the inner muscles in the lower abdominal region, called the *tanden* (丹田), which is the source of energy and the storage place for ki. In yoga and Zen, they may teach you that ki flow is opposite between male and female. They may be correct, but I have not seen enough evidence to convince me that this is so. Therefore, my advice at this time is that you try to rotate your ki toward the direction you feel comfortable or feel "right." If you have not developed a ki flow that is strong enough and cannot feel the difference, then you can try one way and then reverse it after a while. My belief is that the rotation and smooth movement of ki is important, and I do not think the direction will make that much difference.

OK, so you may wonder why the development of ki has to come with breathing, particularly deep breathing. First, let's see if deep breathing is considered to be beneficial in the Western world. Believe it or not, if you Google it, you will see many related articles and sites listing the benefits. One article is on the motivation and awareness site *One Powerful Word*, which lists eighteen benefits of deep breathing:

1. Breathing Detoxifies and Releases Toxins
2. Breathing Releases Tension
3. Breathing Relaxes the Mind/Body and Brings Clarity
4. Breathing Relieves Emotional Problems
5. Breathing Relieves Pain
6. Breathing Massages Your Organs
7. Breathing Increases Muscle
8. Breathing Strengthens the Immune System
9. Breathing Improves Posture
10. Breathing Improves Quality of the Blood
11. Breathing Increases Digestion and Assimilation of Food
12. Breathing Improves the Nervous System
13. Breathing Strengthens the Lungs
14. Proper Breathing Makes the Heart Stronger
15. Proper Breathing Assists in Weight Control
16. Breathing Boosts Energy Levels and Improves Stamina
17. Breathing Improves Cellular Regeneration
18. Breathing Elevates Moods

Enough benefits? Access the full article here: http://www.onepowerfulword. com/2010/10/18-benefits-of-deep-breathing-and-how.html.

It is true that the editor of this site is not a medical person. So, let's check what the medical experts say about deep breathing. I am listing only one of them here, but you can check the Internet and find many other similar sites. The site I am referring to is called *Women to Women: Changing Women's Health—Naturally* by Marcelle Pick, OB/GYN NP. On one page, she writes,

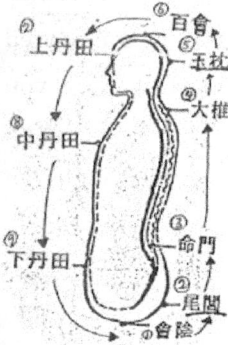

In a 2005 review and analysis of several studies, Richard Brown, MD and Patricia Gerberg, MD reported that yogic deep-breathing techniques were extremely effective in handling depression, anxiety, and stress-related disorders. These techniques can serve as an excellent adjunct to conventional medical treatment—or in some cases as a suitable substitute—in treating myriad psychological disorders, as well as eating disorders and obesity.

If you are interested, you can read the entire article here: http://www.womentowomen.com/fatigueandstress/deepbreathing.aspx.

So, the modern medical society also acknowledges the benefits of deep breathing. It is a shame that it is not popular among average people, including athletes. It is a greater shame that not many karate instructors emphasize the importance of deep breathing or incorporate it in their syllabus. Anyway, Asian people have known of these benefits for centuries and have incorporated deep breathing into different training methods. We believe that ki must be activated and circulated throughout our body to produce positive results, and this is why the deep-breathing method has been used to energize circulation. It is like when you boil water in a teakettle. As you heat the kettle from the bottom, the water circulates up and then rotates and comes down. You can have that image with the ki in your body. Breathing does two things. One is to assist the ki in circulating (internal); the other is to give an energy source (air) to the remote parts of your body (external). The latter is done by blood circulation, but deep breathing will help it by increasing the intake of oxygen and the discharge of carbon dioxide.

OK then, you may wonder where the ki travels in our body. Chinese experts developed a meridian chart called *keiraku* (経絡) to show the system and its exact routes (see illustration right). There is much debate among Western medical personnel about the existence of such paths or routes because no physical organs are visible or detectable as they are in the circulatory system or the nervous system. The *keiraku* was developed by the physical experiences of acupuncture and moxibustion experts over thousands of years.

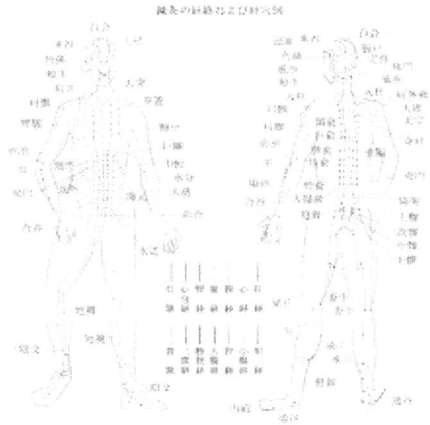

The smooth flow of your ki is the key to your health and life strength. Slow and deep breathing coordinated with slow physical movement will aid and promote circulation. I repeat that this is the reason why I have mentioned that *tai chi chuan* is one of the best methods to develop your ki out of all the martial arts systems (provided that you agree to include it in this category).

Then, you will naturally want to know about karate. Yes, it is about time to talk about our karate training, but what do you think? Unfortunately, the training syllabus includes specific breathing exercises or special training for breathing only at a few Shotokan dojo. If this is the case, then you would think of the training that you do with your *kata*. Sadly again, none of the *kata* is taught with proper instruction pertaining to breathing, and few instructors know how to harmonize breathing with the *kata* movements. The only visible breathing *kata* we have in Shotokan, namely, Hangetsu, lost most of its breathing-method teaching many years ago. Kanazawa Sensei and I are the only ones who do such teaching. In addition, this *kata* almost lost not only its breathing method but also its most important key point, the *hangetsu dachi*. I wrote about this in *Shotokan Myths* (Chapter 11: "Han-

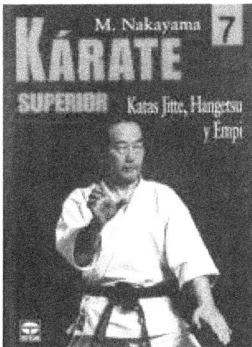

getsu"), so the reader may remember. I have put an instructional video of Hangetsu on the Karate Coaching video site (www.karatecoaching.com), where I explain how it should be done and include a few different breathing methods.

You are familiar with the *kiai* (気合), which you do frequently in your training. It literally means 'to gather or collect ki'. Doesn't this help develop ki? How ironic can it be! The consistent or excessive use of the *kiai*, believe it or not, prevents ki from flowing. It may be a shocking statement, but it is true. A loud *kiai* means a loss of energy, and it disrupts the flow of ki as your body needs to tense up. It is like a loud sound when a bomb explodes. Such a sound does not aid power; rather, energy is wasted as it is an escaped energy. So, if a sound comes out from a powerful technique (like the loud sound from a dynamite explosion), then that is OK, but making a loud *kiai* for its own sake is simply a waste of energy. Maybe it is OK for the children's class so that they can learn to have spirit or let their energy out as they are full of energy. I also wrote in *Shotokan Myths* (Chapter 5: "Silent Kiai") that there was no *kiai* in ancient *kata* or during training on Okinawa prior to the twentieth century. Even Funakoshi did not emphasize the *kiai*, and doing one or two *kiai* in a *kata* was optional (you may want to reread *Karate Do Kyohan*). It all changed when *kata* became a tournament event where some strict rules were needed to judge. Is all *kiai* bad? No, as I said earlier, it is all right if it is done correctly. It can bring extraordinary power to a technique, and I do not mean a magical power. It is difficult to explain with words, but a correct *kiai* will act as a connecting point that brings all the muscle energy together harmoniously from the different parts of the body. This is why the tension of the body, or *kime* (極め), must be a hundredth or even a thousandth of a second. This is true *kime*, and it can be seen in *hakkei* (発勁), translated only as 'explosive power', which is supposed to be a secret or an ultimate technique of kung fu training. This is the energy used in the one-

inch or zero-inch punch. You can see my demonstration of the one-inch punch
on the Karate Coaching video.

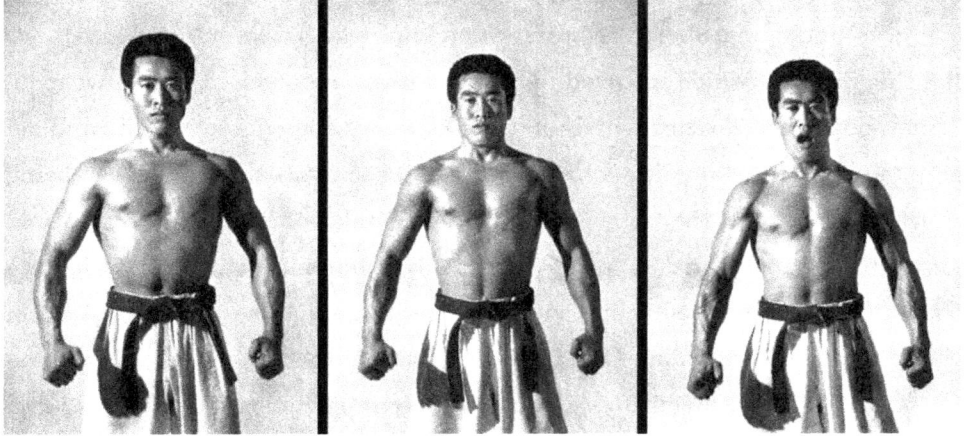

Then, how about *ibuki* (息吹き), the breathing used in Goju Ryu and other
Okinawan styles? I have only limited experience with Goju Ryu training, so I
am not an expert in this style, and I welcome input from Goju Ryu experts. My
understanding is that there are two parts to the objectives of *ibuki*. One is used
in Sanchin (三戦) *kata*, which aims to coordinate body movements with breathing. The other concept is similar to tai chi, but there is a big difference, namely,
that in tai chi, the idea is to relax the muscles, but in Goju Ryu, a practitioner
learns how to tense his body. So, the blocking and punching arms in Sanchin
kata move slowly, but there seems to be too much tension throughout the body,
which slows circulation of the ki in your body. The purpose of this *kata* and the
original Hangetsu was not to aid circulation but maybe only to strengthen the
local ki.

Another training method of *ibuki* is done with the practitioner standing
still while doing heavy breathing (fast inhaling and slow and forced exhal-
ing). The instructor checks the practitioner's tension by punching and kicking
him pretty hard. The idea, I understand, is that the Goju Ryu practitioner
will turn the body to withstand the hits and kicks of an opponent. Obviously,

this concept comes from a short-distance fighting method and is based on the situation of a fist-to-fist-only fight. On Okinawa, all weapons (swords, knives, etc.) were banned for hundreds of years, so this concept could be considered. Shuri Te, including Shorin Ryu and Shotokan, was based on a long-distance fighting method, which involved fighting against an opponent with a weapon. This is one of the reasons why Funakoshi did not adopt *ibuki* training and de-emphasized it in Hangetsu *kata*. The other reason was the way it was being practiced, i.e., with the upper body naked. Funakoshi knew that this would not go too well with the Japanese culture as only manual laborers would take their top off. He wanted to introduce karate into Japan as the martial art of the samurai or gentleman. One great benefit of *ibuki*, however, is its training of the diaphragm. During *ibuki*, you have to pay much attention to your diaphragm and its actions. You learn how to "push down" and "pull up" the diaphragm while you control and manage your breathing. However, this exercise is also practiced in yoga, and I like their exercises more as they are done with much less tension. In addition, their training incorporates moving the internal organs (up and down or in a circular direction) along with the deep breathing. This exercise is excellent for circulating your ki, and it will help you with your health. I recommend this exercise strongly, and I hope the reader will try it.

Back to *kime*. Extended *kime*, or tension, of the muscles is not good for ki flow, and you can read about this in the first chapter of *Shotokan Myths* ("Kime"). To develop ki flow in your karate training, you need to learn how to relax more while you are training. If you enjoy tension in your training, then I recommend that you have a separate session for breathing exercises. I have explained how to do long and deep breathing in my blog. There are other ways to develop ki, and I will include them in my longer version of this subject.

Now that you know how to exercise using a long-and-deep-breathing method, let me conclude this chapter with the highest level of benefits that can come from strong ki and healthy ki flow developed through deep-breathing exercises.

You will be able to control your heartbeat and blood pressure. You will have a stronger immune system. What does this mean? The result is that you will have a very healthy life. Funakoshi boasted when he was in his seventies and early eighties that he never got sick. He credited this to his karate training, which I endorse. He lived to be eighty-eight years old, which was an amazing longevity in that era. He even went through wartime in Tokyo in the 1940s, where food was scarce and sanitation was extremely poor. I agree with Master Funakoshi, and I will write a separate piece on how karate training can produce good health. The more I practice karate, the more I realize how amazingly human beings are created and that our potential is almost unlimited. So, wouldn't you be happy if you simply did not get sick even when you are in your seventies and eighties? You can achieve that level of health with deep breathing and karate training.

You will also be able to control your brain waves at will and your emotional state much better than nonpracticed people. Don't you want to have the abil-

Brain Waves Graph

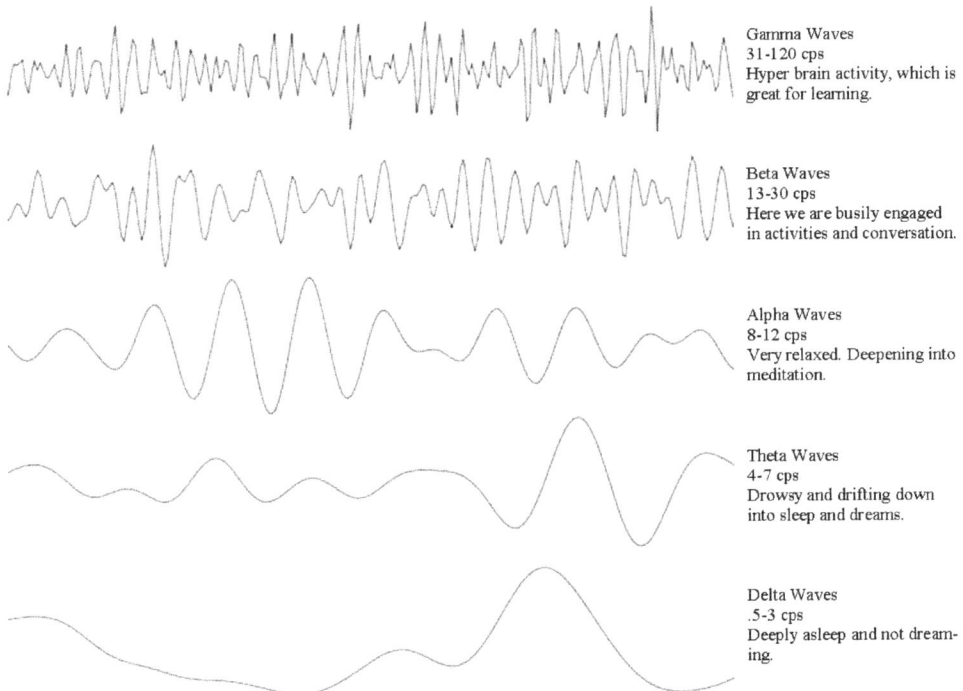

Gamma Waves
31-120 cps
Hyper brain activity, which is great for learning.

Beta Waves
13-30 cps
Here we are busily engaged in activities and conversation.

Alpha Waves
8-12 cps
Very relaxed. Deepening into meditation.

Theta Waves
4-7 cps
Drowsy and drifting down into sleep and dreams.

Delta Waves
.5-3 cps
Deeply asleep and not dreaming.

ity to keep calm and collected when under heavy stress or in emergency situations? You can do this if you can keep your brain waves in relaxed mode. By
having strong ki, you will not be depressed and will be influenced less by bad
or sad news or incidents. This will certainly enable you to have a happier life.

Your mental alertness will improve with better breathing and stronger ki.
What does this mean? You will be able to avoid accidents while you walk, run,
ride a bike, drive, or whatever activities you may do. Out of all the accidents
you may encounter, an automobile accident could be the most serious and the
one you want to avoid the most.

CHAPTER EIGHT
第八章

KI EXCHANGE WITH THE TREES
樹林気功とは

癒し体験 2
Healing experience

樹林気功

I wrote about ki in the previous chapter, and I defined it as "the source or the energy that gives life." We also reviewed that the universe itself is composed of pure energy as matter is energy (Einstein's $E=mc^2$). This means energy is all around us in different forms and on different levels.

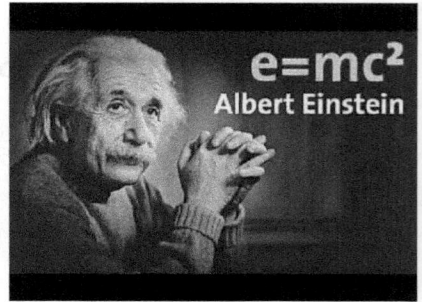

We Asian people have been doing ki exchange with the trees for many centuries. Some people misunderstand that, by this exchange, people are taking energy off from the tree. I do not know how serious one reader was, but he called it a "vampire act." But, he was totally wrong. Ki is like love, so the more you give, the more you will have. By facing a tree, you only exchange ki; you don't take ki away from it. In fact, you send your ki to the tree—pick an old and healthy-looking one—and the tree will purify it, reenergize it, and then return it to you. This is similar to the air exchange you do with the trees. Your lung cells give off carbon dioxide and keep oxygen. As you know, plants take the carbon dioxide you exhaled and emit the oxygen that you will breathe in. A tree does a similar exchange with your ki. This is a full circle of nature, and this is why you will feel that you gained new energy. For those who are skeptical about ki and ki exchange, read the following article from *The Mind Unleashed*, titled "Tree Hugging Now Scientifically Validated": http://www.the-mindunleashed.org/2013/07/tree-hugging-now-scientifically.html.

If you have visited China or Taiwan, you might have seen many Chinese people gathered in a park early in the morning. With a lot of trees around, they go through the slow movements of tai chi training. They do not do this

among the trees because they need shade. As they practice tai chi in the woods, they are, in fact, gaining ki from training with slow abdominal breathing and also from exchanging ki with the trees around them.

Ki exchange can be done not only with a tree but also with many other natural things, such as a mountain, a river, a waterfall, a lake, the ocean, or the sun, as they all have lots of energy. You can exchange or intake ki, or energy, but you also have to be careful how you do the ki exchange with strong sources, such as a volcanic mountain or the sun. Ki exchange with a tree is the most popular because the ki from a tree is mild, and a tree is the easiest thing to find as an exchange partner.

Chinese people train in tai chi early in the morning. It is not because they need to go to work afterwards (most of them are retired old people anyway). They train early in the morning because they know that the ki in the morning has more energy because of the sun, which gives off mild energy in the early morning. For many people, it is more challenging to find the energy to train in the early morning, but it is much healthier to do training in the early morning than to do it at night. Your body is still asleep, so the slow-movement exercise of tai chi is perfect to start your day as it will awaken you with an added ki energy. Chinese people have known about this for thousands of years, and now it has almost become a national event.

I will give you step-by-step instructions on how to exchange ki with a tree. It is not too difficult, but it would help you to know some key points. Before we go into the ki exchange, I want to talk about how trees (and other natural things) are considered in Asia, particularly in Japan. When you visit Japan, take a walk to an old shrine. It may be difficult to find one in Tokyo, but you can try Meiji Shrine or Yasukuni Shrine. If you are lucky enough to visit Kyoto or other smaller cities, you can find them rather easily.

You may find a tree in the yard of a shrine (sometimes on a mountain away

from a shrine) with a paper ribbon or a decoration (see photo left). This means that this particular tree is holy or has strong ki. People either pray to it or try to capture the ki from it. It is not simple idolatry as we (or some of us) can feel the special energy emitted by certain trees. It is typically an old tree, but it is not because of the age alone. There may be other trees that may be bigger and older, but a Shinto priest detected a special tree with his reception of ki.

You may also find a huge rock or a waterfall with some paper and a rope decoration (*shimenawa* [しめ縄]) as shown in the photos on the right and below. These were also selected by the Shinto priests for having strong ki.

It is very interesting to remember that, at my dojo in Japan, we had a winter camp at a waterfall when the water was almost frozen. When I participated years ago, I believed it was only to test our endurance in the cold. But, now I know I was wrong. It was also to gain ki from the waterfall. Our summer camp was at the beach when the temperature went up to over 100°F (40°C). The sand was so hot that it was almost impossible to stand on. We were so happy to

get into the ocean. I thought the practicing of punches and kicks in the waves was to train our stances, but I was wrong. We were to gain ki from the ocean. Even though we were not aware of it, I am sure those trainings were good for our ki.

OK, let's go into ki-exchange training with a tree, *jurin kiko* (樹林気功). First, let me say this. You are not taking energy from the tree. As I use the word *ex-*

change, you are exchanging (taking and returning) ki with the tree, and you are not like a vampire sucking off the energy from the tree. Some people misunderstand this exercise, so I want to explain that this process is more like a filtering of your ki through the tree to purify it. If you pick a healthy and stable tree, it can regenerate your ki, so to speak. So, you almost feel as if you gained more ki, but, in fact, it is different. Now, let me give you the detailed steps and the explanation for each step to exchange ki with a tree.

Step 1: Finding Your Partner

Search for a tree to do a ki exchange with as you go into a park or a wooded area. You need to look for a healthy one and try to open your heart as you look for the tree. It is almost like looking for a friend. Feel the ki of each tree and find the one that reaches out to you. If you open your mind, you can feel it. However, if you do not feel an invitation from any tree, then look for one that is attractive to you. If you often camp out and spend time in nature, I am sure you understand what I am trying to say. You can do the exchange alone (Photo 1), with a group (Photo 2), or with many people spread out (Photo 3 on next page).

1

2

3

Step 2: Positioning

In Japan, we bow to our partner, the tree, before we start our ki exchange. If you feel stupid bowing to a tree, you can start with a simple greeting to the tree. OK, for the reader, after finding your "partner," you will reach out to the tree with your hands. You can put your hands around the tree, point your palms toward it, or even touch it with your hands. It is all up to you, and you can choose any of these approaches that you feel most comfortable with. Then, you stand naturally in *shizentai*(自然体, 'natural stance'), and your body

should be totally relaxed. You are not there to suck up all the energy from the tree. You are there to exchange and to circulate your energy, so relaxation is a must. You can keep your eyes open or closed. Some people prefer keeping their eyes closed so that they can focus their attention on the exchange process or the circulation of ki. If you can detect or notice the feelings of the tree before the ki exchange, then your exchange exercise will surely be successful.

Step 3: Commencing Exchange

So, you are standing next to the tree with your arms extended toward it. Your hands are used either to send out your ki or to receive the ki from the tree. Stand with your body totally relaxed and focus only on sending and receiving ki. This process is not a hard exchange, as in volleyball, tennis, or Ping-Pong, but more like a slow breathing where ki goes in and out instead of air.

When you are feeling strong, you can emit your ki into the tree, and it will send it back to you with more energy or happier energy. You will receive this refreshed ki all through your body, and you will feel as if you could almost jump with the energy. When you are feeling weak, or when you are sick, and your body needs ki, you use your hands to take in or inhale the ki from the tree. In other words, you feel as if you were breathing in the ki through your palms. Then, you breathe out your old or bad ki into the ground through your feet. The tree will take in your ki through the ground and purify it for you. It works much better if you do this with deep breathing from the *tanden* ('lower stomach'). With this breathing, you can rotate the ki in your body as you receive the purified ki.

During the exchange process, you may feel love toward the tree from inside your heart or you may feel that you are receiving it from the tree. I have seen some practitioners cry for joy. If you are lucky to feel its love, you can give it a hug at the end of the session before you leave. You can also say thanks to your "partner" for the ki exchange. I hope you can feel that this tree is also alive and is a part of your life. During the process, you can adjust the distance of your hands from the tree. I keep my hands about thirty centimeters or so from the tree, but you can set your own distance. It really does not matter how close or far away you are, but you will find a comfortable distance for you as you do the exchange many times. I usually do not touch the tree because the sensation of the tree bark dulls the feeling in my palms.

Step 4: Exchanging

You will continue the ki exchange for the duration you wish to spend. You can do it for only ten minutes to an hour or even longer. You can take a break and find another tree if you feel you want to do more. During a ki-exchange session, most people stand still to focus their attention on the ki exchange. I sometimes walk around the tree almost like dancing while waving my hands. If you can synchronize your breathing to your footsteps, it will become like doing a *kata* around the tree, and then you can understand how the tai chi practitioners are receiving ki every morning. I even turn around and expose my back to the tree for full exposure. I try to inhale the ki from my back up through my spine and let it travel upward to my head.

Some people believe that by touching the tree, they can get more or stronger ki. The person in the photo to the left is touching her head to the tree to receive strong ki in hopes of relieving her headache. I am not an expert on this, but I am not sure if she can receive stronger ki by doing this. In my case, I can feel more ki by not touching the tree. So, I guess it is up to the individual to determine which method works best for him.

Step 5: Finishing and Disengaging

Engaging is important, but the finishing stage is also very important, and you must not make it abrupt or impersonal. Slowly open your eyes if they are closed. If you enjoyed the exchange, your face must have a natural smile on it. Relax your arms more and lower them as you disengage the link with the tree. Do not step away or turn around right away or quickly. This is the same as *zanshin* in *kata* or letting go of your loved one or a close friend after a tender hug. You must have that moment of complete closure. You must stand there for fifteen to thirty seconds, looking at the tree with your gratitude and possibly affection. You could thank it and tell it that you enjoyed it or that you will come back. We Japanese will bow before we step away from the tree. If you can feel affection or friendship toward the tree, as I suggested earlier, you can hug the tree as you would do to your friend. I sometimes tap or pet the tree to thank it before I bow to it as I say goodbye. I can almost guarantee you that it will be one of the most enjoyable encounters and that you will feel a unification with nature.

Ki has been mentioned by many of the *budo* masters, such as Ueshiba (aikido [photo right]), Funakoshi (Shotokan), Uehara (Motobu Ryu), Hatsumi (ninjutsu), and Asai (Asai Ryu), as being a very important part of the martial arts. Thus, developing ki is extremely important in *bujutsu* karate. It also helps your mental and physical health. So, I recommend that all karate practitioners try this exercise to feel your ki. You have nothing to lose by trying this. Even if you cannot feel the exchange or the ki itself, at least you will have an enjoyable and relaxing time in the woods. So, why not try this ki exchange with a tree the next time you visit the park?

CHAPTER NINE
第九章

WHAT IS "COMPLETE" SELF-DEFENSE?
完全なる護身とは何ぞや？

Self-defense—this term is very popular, and we as karate practitioners are all familiar with this concept. So, why am I writing a chapter about this subject, which is apparently not a mystery?

I am happy to explain the meaning of this subject because I feel something important is being missed. I have noticed that there is a big gap between what the general public believes and what the full meaning of self-defense really is. What concerns me more is that I get the feeling that the majority of karate practitioners also seem to accept the general belief about self-defense. It is my grave fear that, for this reason, many karate practitioners may not be receiving the full potential benefit of true self-defense from their daily karate training. I can almost hear the loud disagreement from the reader: "Hey what do you mean? Our practice includes both *bunkai* and in-depth self-defense techniques. I can handle an attacker in a dark alley."

Great...but, unfortunately, this very mind-set is exactly what I am talking about and is the reason for me to write this chapter. So, my claim is that one is missing a lot if he believes the main purpose and objective of karate training is to defend oneself from an attacker in a dark alley or a bar or wherever else. I even have to say that one may be wasting his training if he cannot acquire the rest of the benefits. Yes, the term *waste* that I use here may be a surprising word for the reader, but I feel strongly enough about this to use this word. Do you realize that defending yourself against an attacker in a dark alley is only one side of the coin, so to speak, when you consider all the benefits you can get from total self-defense? Without attaining the benefits from both sides of the coin, you could be wasting your karate training.

If we can define what *total self-defense* really means, then it will naturally reveal what the other side of the coin entails. So, we should step back now and check out the standard definition of *self-defense*. The best way to get that is

probably to check what is written in *Wikipedia*. Here is the link to this subject: http://en.wikipedia.org/wiki/Self_defense. Let me quote from the page here:

Self-defense...is a countermeasure that involves defending the well-being of oneself or of another from harm. The use of the right of self-defense as a legal justification for the use of force in times of danger is available in many jurisdictions, but the interpretation varies widely.

This is a very concise and short explanation. It adds some subtopics to explain further. It lists "Physical" as a section and explains, "Physical self-defense is the use of physical force to counter an immediate threat of violence." Then, it lists the sections "Unarmed" and "Armed." Martial arts is included under "Unarmed." Under "Armed," of course, it lists many weapons. *Wikipedia* continues with "Other forms", which are "Avoidance," "De-escalation," and "Personal alarms." I am sure you understand what is entailed in the first two. The last one is interesting as it refers to a personal alarm, which it defines as a "small, hand-held device that emits strong, loud, high-pitched sounds." Most readers have this device with their car key.

Thirdly, they list "Mental" to complete all the aspects of self-defense. This section starts with the following sentence: "Mental self-defense is the ability to get into the proper mind-set for executing a physical self-defense technique." It further explains the importance of this aspect in the same context. The context and the thought pattern are the same as in "Physical." It lacks the aspect of the self. This shows the same attitude or mind-set of people in general. I will explain in this chapter that this is missing the other half, which is very important.

Wikipedia also includes "Self-defense education" and "Legal aspects." Both are interesting, especially the second one. California and a few other states consider nunchaku to be an illegal weapon, but I will not go into this here.

You can summarize that *self-defense* refers to the idea of defending oneself (which includes protecting family and material things that belong to him or them) from other people. I suspect many practitioners must have started karate training with the hope of learning self-defense abilities. There is nothing wrong with that, and we should keep this mind-set in our karate training, too. It is a shame that we have to watch out not only for criminals

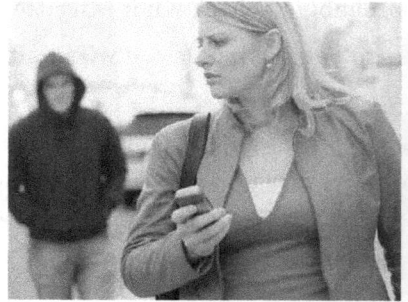

and strangers but also for friends, relatives, and spouses, unfortunately. In addition to physical attacks, we also need to consider verbal attacks and other attacks that affect us psychologically, emotionally, and even financially. I am sure I do not need to go into the details as all of us are familiar with the various situations and cases that require some measures to defend ourselves. I strongly recommend de-escalation techniques and passive self-defense tools (such as alarm bells) that can be learned or carried. There are many specific programs, such as self-defense for women, children, and senior citizens, and there are even programs for self-defense against verbal attacks. I respect these programs, and there is definitely a place for them. I am skeptical, however, as to whether karate ability could help in a real life-or-death situation, especially if an attacker has a lethal weapon, such as a knife or a gun. I prefer to put more value and emphasis on some other ability you could gain in karate training, such as alertness or confidence, rather than on the actual karate techniques to fight an assailant. Staying calm and using a commonsense approach tends to result in a better outcome when you face a mugger or a robber.

Unless you live in a slum area or a third-world country where robbery with a gun is very common, the possibility of facing a robber with a gun may only be once in your lifetime. If you wish to subdue such an attacker, I would not recommend karate training at all. I suggest that you hand over your wallet or even your car to stay safe. No worldly possession is worth your life. However, if you do not wish to hand over your wallet or your car, then I suggest you carry a gun. I personally oppose gun ownership, but that is another subject. Though this is a controversial subject, and much can be discussed about it, I will proceed to the main subject of this chapter.

So, what I have discussed above is only one side of the complete self-dense issue, but there is another side. I consider this flip side to be more important, and it must receive more attention. The concept I will share should not be that difficult or foreign to the reader. However, it is rarely considered to be a part of self-defense by most of the public and, unfortunately, by many karate practitioners, as well. OK, that is enough of an introduction. What is the other side? Who is our greatest enemy? The answer is simple; it is ourself. Yes, that is correct, ourself. What we need to do here is shift our attention from the attacker in a dark alley to the hazards and incidents caused by our own actions. To complete our self-defense, we must have a strategy to prevent these things. There are two major areas of self-caused hazards. We will examine each of them and check why they are ignored. I will then present what can be done about them.

The first one entails both the physical and the mental health aspect. (There is also a spiritual aspect, but we will focus on the first two in this chapter.) This is a big subject, and we will take a look at it more closely in the first part of this chapter. The other area involves self-inflicted accidents, including automobile collisions, slipping/falling, sports-related accidents, and other accidents.

Let's face it; we are more dangerous to ourselves than a mugger in a dark alley or a drunk in a bar. We hurt ourselves more frequently and possibly do more damage to ourselves. This can be prevented or avoided, and that would complete our self-defense. Even though the problems from this side are more pervasive and common, they are rarely considered to be matters of self-defense that can be and need to be managed. Furthermore, we do not tie karate training and discipline to this concept.

Let me start with the subject of health. I am sure you agree that health is an important subject. At the same time, you may believe that sickness comes from outside, like a mugger in a dark alley, and that we are helpless victims. Or, you may also believe that we have no control over illness and that catching a cold once a year is normal and cannot be helped. You may not agree with me, but I believe that most sickness is self-inflicted or self-caused. Though in most cases it is not intentional, in some cases it is intentional but not realized. Statistics show that most sick calls to the workplace are reported on Mondays.

Once we get seriously ill, we may have to spend many days in the hospital, which is very inconvenient and can also be very costly. If we know this acutely, then why not spend more time and attention on preventing or avoiding sickness? Yes, if you go to your dojo three times per week, then you are doing a positive thing for your health, but this is only the start and is not enough. I have written an article about seven tips for good health in the past. I described my ideas and recommendations to make you healthy or healthier. By reading that article, you can complete your understanding of this subject. There are two parts to health: the physical and the mental. These two parts are closely intertwined and integrated; thus, they should be considered two sides of the same coin. However, for this chapter, I will discuss them separately and reserve the integration project for the future.

Let us start with the physical side of health.

When we talk about our body, we must be aware of the five major flows in our body. You know them, but how often do we pay enough attention to their functions and their affect on our health? Probably not too often.

Here they are:

1. Blood circulation
2. Respiration
3. Digestion
4. Excretion
5. Ki circulation

I am aware that there are other flow systems in our body, such as body temperature, hormone level and heartbeat (pulse), but they are kept fairly constant, so I did not include them in the list despite their smaller scale of flows and rhythms.

I do not think I need to explain each of the five items above. I suspect that you are familiar with all of them except possibly for Number 5, ki circulation. If you do not believe ki exists, just consider the electrical static flow that can be shown as brain waves or electrocardiography, normally referred to as *EKG* or *ECG*, which is used to determine heart problems. Here is the *Wikipedia* page for electrocardiography to learn more about it: http://en.wikipedia.org/wiki/Electroencephalography.

The point I want to make here is that to keep our body healthy, we must keep the flow of all these systems smooth and continuous. The easiest one to control and manage is breathing (respiration). If it is suspended for more than five minutes, you know for sure what the consequence will be. You must breathe several times per minute to stay alive.

The other is blood circulation. Your heart pumps diligently without stopping throughout your life. If it ever stops, it means the end of your life. We eat food three times every day and go to the toilet daily. As you think about them, you can see, and possibly feel, the flows in your body, and, hopefully, you agree that they are important to your health.

Keeping a smooth and fluid circulation of these five flows will contribute greatly to your health. This concept is well expressed by the Asian wisdom of yin and yang (陰陽 [photo right]). One must know that a slower flow is better than a faster one. I have spoken in another chapter about deep breathing (slow breathing) and its importance and good effect on the heart and health in general.

To have smooth digestion, naturally moderating your eating and making a habit of eating at certain times is important. If you eat too much, your body will tell you with certain symptoms, such as heartburn or extra secretions of stomach acid.

The excretion part of the flow is not a pleasant topic, and many people tend to ignore it, but it is extremely important for our health. Constipation is a very common problem among women. A correct diet with natural fibers will solve most cases. Popular fast foods certainly do not help this trend.

Regarding the last item, ki, you can probably understand better if I tell you that meditation will help you with your emotions and peace of mind. Meditation provides a harmonizing and calming effect on the brain waves. I have also mentioned that deep breathing will help with the calming of the mind. These are all connected and tied together. When you observe the whole system and understand how they work, it will all make sense to you.

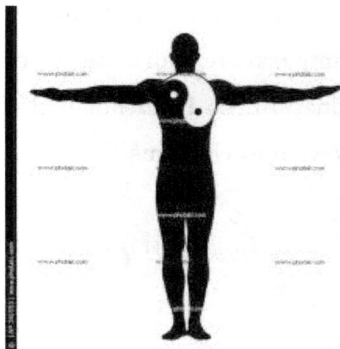

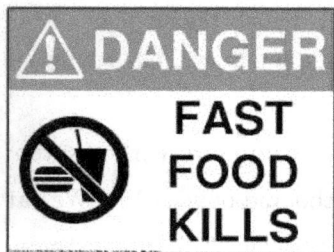

There are several things that are recommended for your health, such as correct diet, proper exercise, getting enough rest and sleep, taking supplements, and regulating lifestyle (setting a time to get up, go to sleep, and eat all three meals). I will not go into these items as it would expand this chapter into a book. I will cover these items when I write a new article on the health issue. In addition to the recommended items, there are things we must avoid or minimize. They are smoking, alcohol consumption, unhealthy diet (soft drinks, processed food, and the "McDiet"), obesity, irregular lifestyle, and many more that I will not list in this chapter.

If you are truly interested in complete self-defense, then you will want to know all the details, and you will implement them. By doing all that is recommended and avoiding that which is not healthy, you will strengthen the immune system in your body. Even if you encounter the flu virus, you will not catch a cold as your immune system will take care of it. You may be exposed to extra pollen in the spring, but you will not suffer from hay fever because your well-functioning body system will not overreact to the environment. On the other hand, doing the opposite, such as having poor eating habits with an unhealthy diet, smoking, drinking too much alcohol, being overweight, etc., causes your body's harmony to get unbalanced, and your immune system becomes weakened. In this condition, many different viruses can affect your system. You will catch a cold every winter; you will have an allergy every spring. In addition, you may not be able to sleep well at night, or you could get an upset stomach after each meal.

You may say, "OK, these may be good hints and ideas, but what do they have to do with my karate training?" The key words here are *will power* and *discipline*. We learn discipline in our dojo, and now we must expand it to our daily life and all the things we do every day. This is exactly what Funakoshi was trying to tell us in his *Niju Kun*: "Karate goes beyond the dojo," and, "Apply the way of karate to all things. Therein lies its beauty." Please, ask yourself if you are applying the will power and

一、空手は礼に始まり礼に終る事を忘るな
二、空手に先手なし
三、空手は義の補け
四、先づ自己を知れ而して他を知れ
五、技術より心術
六、心は放たん事を要す
七、禍は懈怠に生ず
八、道場のみの空手と思ふな
九、空手の修業は一生である
十、凡ゆるものを空手化せよ其処に妙味あり
十一、空手は湯の如し絶えず熱を与えざれば元の水に還る
十二、勝つ考は持つな負けぬ考は必要
十三、敵に因って転化せよ
十四、戦は虚実の操縦如何に在り
十五、人の手足を劍と思へ
十六、男子門を出づれば百万の敵あり
十七、構は初心者に後は自然体
十八、型は正しく実戦は別物
十九、力の強弱体の伸縮技の緩急を忘るな
二十、常に思念工夫せよ

空手二十箇條
船越義豪遺訓

discipline that you learned in the dojo to your daily life. An in-depth explana-tion of the *Niju Kun* can be found in the last chapter of this book.

Another person may ask and complain, "You listed so many things to do and not to do. I can understand that we must not smoke and must stay away from the Big Mac, but you talk about taking supplements, the immune system, brain waves, and so many other things. Aren't there too many for a regular practitioner to cover them all?" Yes, if you try to cover them in one day or even in one week, maybe you will not be able to cover them all. You need to expand your time to months and years. Then you can cover them all. When you talk about the other self-defense, you think about many different situations and conditions. I am sure most readers have seen the self-defense demonstrations where they exhibit many different situations, including being grabbed in many different ways, having an arm or both arms twisted, sitting down, defending against different weapons, etc. You do not become an expert in all those situa-tions in a day or a week or even after training for a year. You must practice for many years before you can reach that level. Then, why not with the flip side of self-defense? You have much more time when you are outside of the dojo, so there is no excuse for not having the time. All you need is a desire and a com-mitment to complete your self-defense and become super healthy.

In health, there is another aspect, however, called *mental health*. The feeling of happiness comes from your mind. If you have a negative mind-set or attitude, you tend to be unhappy and dis-satisfied. All of us are under some type of stress in our life, of course, and if we succumb to great stress, then that can cause us to have an illness. As I mentioned earlier, the physical body and the mind are tightly connected, and they influence each other. It is medically proven that your attitude or mind-set affects your immune system. In an article on health, I mentioned several

alternative treatments to cancer. One was laughter therapy, and the other was music therapy. I will not go into the details of these treatments here.

Love and affection are important to keep in good health. All of us agree that our family is important, and a happy family gives us much affection. I am blessed as I have three sons. A member of a karate dojo learns not only respect but also camaraderie among members. We refer to our dojo as a karate family, and the relationship built there is so strong that the friendship can last many decades. Doctors recommend that a single elderly person have a pet, especially a dog, to keep in good health. It is very true and statistically proven that the life expectancy of an older person with a living spouse is longer than that of one who has lost his partner. As I mentioned earlier, the physical and mental parts are closely intertwined. If your body is healthy, then it is easier to feel happy. If you keep a positive attitude, your immune system will stay strong and will sustain your good health.

So, karate discipline, the spirit of *osu*, and a can-do attitude indeed do help in your quest for super health. Your teacher may have told you in the past that you will not be defeated until you give up. Funakoshi also told us in one of his *Niju Kun*, "Do not think of winning. Think, rather, of not losing." So, we must not lose to a negative attitude, stress, bad news, sorrows, etc. It is natural to have emotional ups and downs, but with will power, you can make the waves as small as possible. If you have trained very hard in the dojo, then you will be calm at a tournament match, at a *dan* examination, or even in front of a mugger. The same thing can be said about mind training for your mental health. A true karate expert will not get extremely angry or be defeated by sadness. *Moderation* is the key word in the mind of the karate expert.

The second area you need to pay attention to in your complete self-defense is accidents. This includes slipping/falling, vehicular accidents (e.g., car, motorcycle, bicycle, etc.), incidents in sports activities, and even small things, such as cutting your face while shaving (read Chapter 12: "The Art of Perfect Shaving").

You may believe an unfortunate accident, such as slipping and falling down a staircase or being involved in a car accident, happens because you are simply unlucky, and it cannot be helped. I disagree. By applying your karate expertise, you are able to prevent and avoid almost all accidents. You cannot call yourself an expert if you cannot prevent these accidents. Though you may not like to hear this, you have failed in one of the key aspects of self-defense. My statement is, once again, very controversial, and it may sound extreme. I can almost hear the voice of the disbeliever, but I can confidently tell you that you will be able to avoid almost all of the accidents I listed above once you achieve a true martial arts mind and ability. In other words, you need to take your karate training outside of the dojo and apply the complete self-defense mind-set to your daily activities.

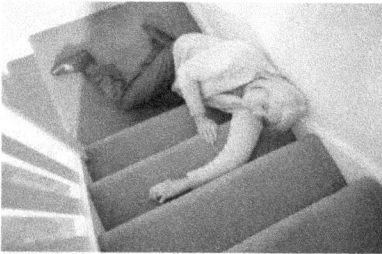

The most dangerous things for senior citizens are not muggers or purse snatchers. What they have to protect themselves from each and every day is car accidents and falls. I have witnessed how serious a fall can be for an aged person through my mother's experience. She was probably one of the most active and healthy people in Japan when she was in her seventies. She practiced yoga and tai chi daily, and she looked twenty years younger than her age. When she hit eighty, I truly believed she would live to be a hundred. Unfortunately, she passed four years ago, and she was only eighty-eight. She fell when she was eighty-three and broke her arm. Then, she fell again when she was eighty-five, and this time she broke her hip. After this accident, her health declined very quickly. She was overconfident as she was carrying shopping bags when she fell; thus, she could not fall correctly. I asked her to use a cane when she walked, but she refused to do so. She walked very slowly without a cane, which reduced her exercise and her tai chi training. Due to her age, I wished she was more humble and more cautious about her safety. But, you know how determined a mother can be. She was a very independent and self-sufficient person, so no one could tell her what to do.

Let me share another story to show you the common mentality of senior citizens. I teach a class at a senior citizens' hall in San Jose. The management requested last year (2012) that I talk to its members about self-defense. They offered me a free lunch with them, so I took the offer. On that day, there were more than twenty members who were all over sixty years old—one was over ninety and in a wheelchair. I started to talk about the most dangerous things for senior citizens, the same things I described above, such as correct diet, car accidents, and falling. They stopped me before I even got through the first ten minutes of my talk. They said, "We are not interested in those things. We want to know if you can teach us a karate technique to fend off muggers and purse snatchers."

So, I told them, "OK, I will teach you a good karate technique for that situation." I continued, "When you meet a mugger, just give him your wallet. If you encounter a purse snatcher, do not resist; let him have it."

The audience protested after a short laugh and asked, "Is this a joke?"

I replied, "No, this is not a joke. This is what I truly recommend."

They looked at each other then said, "Come on, you are a karate sensei. You can teach us a real karate technique."

So, I replied, "Fine, the true karate technique is not to get into that situation. Prevention is the key. Drive extremely carefully or take public transportation whenever possible. Do not walk down the street alone and avoid shopping at night." They did not like my answer at all. At this point, I asked them, "Who takes medication of some kind daily?" All of them raised their hands. I continued, "How many different kinds?" The answers ranged from one kind to more than a dozen different pills. My next question was this: "Do you know what is in those pills? And, do you know exactly what those pills are doing to your body?" None of them could answer.

One guy said, "Hey, these are prescribed by my doctor, and I trust him." I realized that this was the common attitude of the audience. They are not taking charge of their health matters. They go to a doctor, so they believe they are taking care of their health. They say OK to all the shots and pills. The doctors love these patients as this is where they make their money. I am sure most doctors are prescribing these medications, believing that they are good for the patients. At the same time, it is also true that medications are over-prescribed in most of the country. I am not guessing; it is documented. Here is an article from *Enlighten America*, "US Health Statistics: Americans Most Over-Prescribed Country in the World": http://www.enlightenamerica.com/files/Over-Prescribed.pdf.

Read it yourself if you do not believe me. If you Google *overprescription*, you will find 218 million results on this subject, and many of them tell you the facts and the statistics. My last message to the senior-citizen members on that day was this: "Pay more attention to the health matters that are facing you daily instead of worrying about a possible purse snatcher." I do not know how many of them really heard my message, but they realized that one karate teacher was not thinking of kicking and punching when he was talking about self-defense.

How about younger people? I say an automobile accident is the most dangerous and likely accident one can expect in the modern world. Read about this subject in Chapter 11: "Jidosha Dojo (Automobile Studio)." In it I described in detail how to avoid accidents and even traffic tickets. For the younger generation, falling may not be a real threat, but cutting your face while shaving may be a daily irritation. You will enjoy another chapter on this subject, Chapter 12: "The Art of Perfect Shaving."

Conclusion

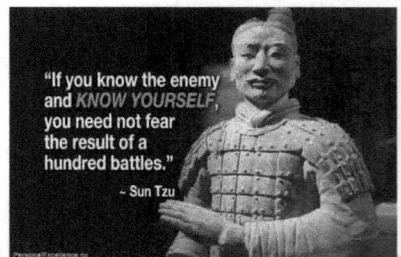

"If you know the enemy and *KNOW YOURSELF*, you need not fear the result of a hundred battles."
– Sun Tzu

Sun Tzu (孫子), a Chinese military general, strategist, and philosopher of the fifth or sixth century B.C., is best known for his book *The Art of War*. His famous quote is this: "If you know the enemy and know yourself, you need not fear the result of a hundred battles." He is right. If we know ourself, then we can avoid almost all accidents and illness. By doing this, you can finally complete your true self-defense training.

CHAPTER TEN
第十章

WHY IS RELAXING OUR MUSCLES SO DIFFICULT?
何故リラックスするのは難しいのか？

Do you get overtensed or uptight at work or in some
situations at home? I am sure you will say, "Yes,
my work is important and is very demanding. I
also worry about all the bills every month, about
my kids, and even about my pets." It is true that
most of us are living in a very stressful society and
a world filled with tensions that bring us stress. We
have so many things we have to worry about and pay attention to just to survive a single day. I know you could probably use a vacation.

There are many methods and ways to help you relax, which include meditation, yoga, massage, classical music, a bath, etc. These are all good and beneficial. I am sure any combination of them will help you relax even more. One
excellent method is progressive muscle relaxation, which is a systematic technique that was developed by Dr. Edmund Jacobson in the 1920s. He discovered
that a muscle could be relaxed by first tensing it for a few seconds and then
releasing it afterward. Dr. Jacobson's technique involves learning to monitor
tension in each specific muscle group in the body by deliberately inducing tension in each group. This tension is then released with attention being paid to
the contrast between tension and relaxation. If you wish to learn more about
this system, a detailed explanation of the steps can be found at AMSA (American Medical Student Association): www.amsa.org.

It is very true that your state of stress and tension has lots to do with your
state of mind. Thus, beautiful music, a pleasant scent, or a scene such as a
beautiful beach or mountains will help you relax. Of course, external stimu-
lants, such as a bath and a massage, will help, too. In addition, moving your
body is a good method to relax, and I am sure you have found this out from
your karate workout. These things are important, but here I am going to shed
a different light on the subject of relaxing.

So, I need to ask you to look at my question again. My question is not why
relaxing is so difficult, though this is also a good question. Rather, I am spe-

cifically asking why it is difficult to relax *our muscles*. Why am I asking this? There are two reasons.

One reason is that I have found so many karate practitioners to be stiff or inflexible. I will soon be sixty-seven years old this year, and I do not consider myself to be flexible, but I am more flexible than most students who are much younger than I. I am not bragging about this as I consider the degree of flexibility I have to be one of the requirements for an instructor. I feel something needs to be done so that more karate practitioners will gain needed flexibility. In addition, I have found the same tendency among our youth. They should be as flexible as a rubber band, but many of them are not. I know we are doing stretches in our karate training, yet with all those exercises to stretch and loosen up, why do we remain somewhat inflexible?

And, the other reason why I am bringing this subject to your attention is certainly not to ridicule or demean practitioners. It is rather because no one else has talked about it, let alone explained it. You can Google this subject and go through many pages, but I bet you cannot find a ready-made answer to this question. I took kiko training under Master Nishino for three years, between 1998 and 2000. I did not learn the technique of punching by using ki; rather, I learned how to relax better. Then, I started to practice under Master Asai and learned how to be more relaxed by observing his moves and techniques. Though he did not teach me the exact method,

I believe I discovered it on my own. I also believe this method changed my karate. Today I am happy to share the concept and the idea of the method that I call *body-core relaxation*.

Though I will mention the bones and cover some physiological subjects, I do not intend to provide a medical explanation, such as how the muscles are constructed and how they work. I am not a medical doctor, so my approach is

somewhat different, and my idea is new. I will present a physiological explanation that a nonmedical person such as I can explain. In addition, not only will
I explain why it is difficult to relax our muscles, but I will also share with the
reader a simple and easy exercise to increase flexibility. I am very confident
that my method will help you not only in your karate training, but also in your
daily life. Yes, it sounds like a TV commercial, but I truly believe in my find-
ings. I will ask you to be the judge and evaluate my presentation to see if you
agree or disagree.

Now, let's get back to the subject of inflexibility. By the way, being inflexible
is nothing to be ashamed of. It is only one of the abilities that are required in
the martial arts, and you can improve it if you know how. When I talk about
inflexible, I am not simply talking about the leg joints. If one can do the splits,
he can kick high and is considered to be flexible. That may be only partially
true. Even a person who can kick high is not considered to be a karate expert if
he can only move in a rigid manner, and his movements are not fluid. The big
question here is how we can attain the ability to make our moves fluid. This is
closely related to the flexibility of our body. It is more than having flexible hip
joints and being able to kick high. I am pretty confident my method will help
and that the result will affect (positively, of course) all of your movements in
your daily activities.

Before we go into my idea and method, let us look at our body. We are under
the false belief that we know about our body since we "live" in it. However, to
our surprise, we discover that most of us do not know or have accurate knowledge of how our body is constructed unless we happen to be in the medical field
or in some scientific field. Our body is covered by skin, so it hides everything
that is inside of our body. We cannot see the bones and the internal organs;
thus, they are there, but they are not visible to our conscious mind. Let's check
and see if you have some essential knowledge about your body.

The following information may not be necessary for beginners or even intermediate students, but it definitely is for advanced students and practitioners.

How many bones do we have in our body? According to the *InnerBody* site (www.innerbody.com), the skeletal system in an adult body is made up of 206 individual bones. The exact number is not important for our discussion as you are not taking a test for your biology class. It is important to know that we do not have only fifty or even a hundred; we have many more. Did you know that the number is more than two hundred? Amazing, huh? Then, how about the number of joints? We need them to move our bones. This question is a little more difficult because the definition of *joint* can be tricky. For instance, the skull is made up of a large number of small bony plates, but they are fused together as a single unit, so they do not account as the joints we are looking for. You can check this on different online sites, and they tell you 340 or even 360 joints. What is important to us is the movable and semimovable joints in our body. We have over 230 of them, and many of them are in our hand (www.drstandley.com).

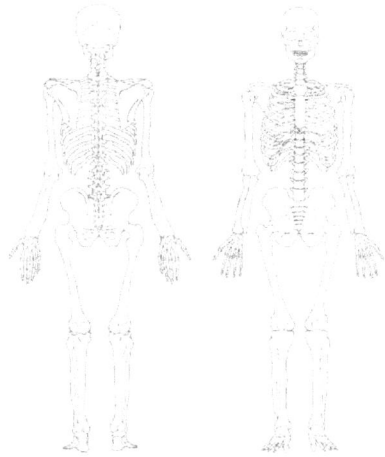

To make our body parts move, we need muscles that pull the bones, using the joints as pivot points. My last question is how many muscles we have in our body. The exact number is difficult to define because different sources group muscles differently, but it is in the range of 640 to 850 (http://en.wikipedia.org/wiki/List_of_muscles_of_the_human_body).

Do not be amazed yet. Let's look at the number of cells we have to build our body. Would you believe that there are 37.2 trillion cells in our body? Yes, trillion, not million or even billion. A trillion is a million times a million. Can you imagine having so many cells, "parts," in your body?

After taking in these figures, I hope you will have a much greater appreciation for the complexity of our body construction and respect for what we are.

Some people have tried to compare our body to a complex racing car or even to something more complex, a jet plane. A Boeing 747 has more than six million parts. When you compare this to the number 37.2 trillion, a jet plane seems to be only a crude toy.

OK, enough of the complexity of our body. Now, when we talk about flexibility, whom do you think of? You may think of someone who is flexible, but, categorically, do you not agree that babies are flexible? I remember that my son's foot could touch his shin as his ankle was so flexible. His foot could touch his ear just like the photo on the right (this is not a photo of my son). At the age of twenty-two, my son now complains that he is stiff and cannot touch his feet with his hands when his legs are straight. What had happened to him? Well, you may say, "Hey, it is only natural. We all get less flexible as we get older." You are right, and this is true. Most senior citizens are very stiff, and their body movements are not fluid at all. But, I knew my teacher, Tetsuhiko Asai, who was featured in the prominent Japanese karate magazine *Karate-Do* for his flexibility.

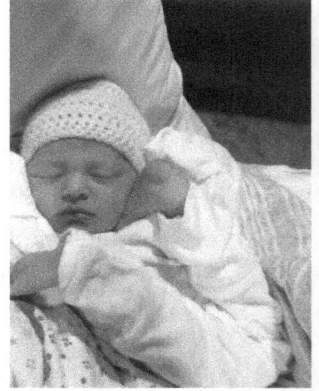

The photo to the left is from the article in that magazine. He was in his late sixties at that time. He kept his flexibility until he passed when he was seventy-one years old. Yes, he was a genius in karate, and we call him *The One and Only*. His moves were powerful yet very fluid. Don't we wish we could move like that? But, are we asking too much? You may think it is impossible for us to get this wish, but my answer is that it is possible to be as flexible as Master Asai. The degrees of flexibility may vary depending on the individual, but becoming more flexible is not impossible at all once you find out how to truly relax your body.

Now let me present my idea as to why we tend to be stiff or get less flexible as we get older. I believe there is a definite reason that goes beyond just age or natural biological causes. When I started my sport science and kinesiology study on my own, I came to realize one very unique thing about us human beings. We are the only animal that is bipedal. In other words, we walk on two legs while many mammals, such as dogs, cats, horses, etc., walk on four legs. Even the closest species, chimpanzees, need to use their arms to walk most of the time. As we have been doing this "trick" called *walking* ever since we were one year old, we do not think this is an amazing or unique act.

I jokingly used the word *trick*, but when you think of what we do, it is really a difficult technique. In fact, it takes months before a baby can walk in a steady manner from the time it learns to stand up. Initially, a baby will take a step or two, then it sits down or falls down. It repeats this task many times every day, then it can walk more than a few steps. Before a baby can walk, it needs to learn how to stand up and keep standing up. A smiling baby who can stand up for the first time is cute. But, did you notice that this baby sways, and you are worried it will fall down? Most of the time it does fall as it is not easy to keep standing up. Even if the baby can keep standing, it does not look steady at all as an adult would. Of course, the baby needs to learn how to balance on two feet. Just think, we are carrying the heaviest part of our body, our head, on top in this balancing act. The simple act of just standing is indeed much more difficult than balancing a baseball bat or an umbrella on your finger. There is an article about standing on *Wikipedia*: http://en.wikipedia.org/wiki/Standing.

Unless you already know the mechanism of standing, I suggest that you read this page and appreciate the delicate and precise body mechanism that is required just to stand. A very important point is this: although seemingly static, our body rocks very slightly back and forth from the ankle in the sagittal plane, one of three planes of our body (http://en.wikipedia.org/wiki/Anatomical_terms_of_location#Planes).

So, you may not notice or be aware of it, but we sway in our quiet standing, albeit within a small range. When we are babies, that sway is much greater, and we notice it. As we get better at controlling our balance, the sway minimizes to a level the people around us, including the person standing next to us, do not notice. As I mentioned earlier, simply standing requires dynamic, rather than static, balance. There are many mechanisms in the body that are required to make adjustments for and to maintain that balance. This is a separate subject, but it is healthier and better if we try to "ride" on this swing or sway rather than stop it. I have already covered this subject in another book that I published, *Shotokan Mysteries*, under Chapter 9: "Unstable Balance." So, I will not go into it in this chapter.

OK, you agree that I made a point that standing does require a fine balancing act. So what? This is the key point, and I wish to explain further, but I need to ask the reader to be patient. I need to detour a little again. Remember one of the examples I mentioned above about the balancing of a baseball bat? Let me ask you which is easier to balance: a bat, which is one piece (as seen in the photo above), or a piece of wood that has, say, twenty pieces that are connected by joints? Of course, we do not have a baseball bat made like that. Below is a photo of wine glasses being

placed on top of each other. So, imagine if what you are trying to balance were made up of, say, five or six wine glasses. I am sure you will say that balancing the glasses is much more difficult than balancing the baseball bat.

Now I want you to look at the bone

structure of our body. I am sure you know
that our body is supported by the bones
in the legs. What is more important is the
bones between the pelvis and the head,
namely, the vertebral column, commonly
called the *backbone* or *spine*. Do you know
how many bones there are to construct this
important body part? It usually consists of
thirty-three (33) vertebrae, but what is im-

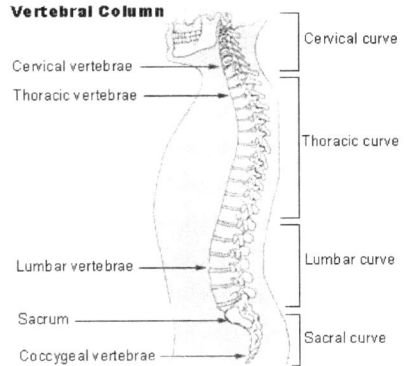

Vertebral Column
Cervical vertebrae
Thoracic vertebrae
Lumbar vertebrae
Sacrum
Coccygeal vertebrae
Cervical curve
Thoracic curve
Lumbar curve
Sacral curve

portant is the upper twenty-four (24) articulating vertebrae that are separated
by discs. For our discussion, I will ignore the lower nine (9) as they are fused
into one piece. There are seven (7) vertebrae in the cervical curve that supports
your head in the neck area. Further down, there are twelve (12) thoracic vertebrae, which make up the upper part of your backbone between the shoulders
and the bottom of the rib cage. Finally, there are five (5) lumbar vertebrae in
the lower back above the pelvis, where many *karateka* complain about a back
pain.

The exact number of vertebrae is not important in our discussion. What
is important is that the spine is not a single piece like a baseball bat. It is
made up of many pieces, and they are connected by discs, or, more accurately,
intervertebral discs. Each disc forms a joint that allows slight movement of the
vertebrae and acts as a ligament to hold the vertebrae together. One crucial
role of the discs is to act as a shock absorber. So, what is important here is that
each vertebra is movable. You can see this easily if you move your head. You
can even rotate your head left and right. You can make similar movements
with the lower back. For instance, you can bend your upper body forward,
backward, and side to side. You can also rotate your upper body even without
moving your pelvis. Try this from a sitting position and you will find out how
flexible or inflexible your thoracic vertebrae are.

We all know that the backbone is important. When you fall off of a horse

or a bike, you may have a spinal cord injury, and some unlucky people may even suffer paralysis below the neck, which will disable them from walking. You remember the famous actor Christopher Reeve, who suffered quadriplegia in 1995 and died in 2004 at the age of fifty-two. Even if the injury is not that serious, we see many people in a neck brace, most of whom suffered from a car accident. These are not directly connected to the subject I am covering, but I just wanted to stress the fact that our head is heavy and that balancing it on top of the spine is not an easy task as it requires a technique that is like a trick.

Now, finally, here is the main point I want to share. Most of us have no recollection of how we tried to stand up and walk when we were a baby. We can guess how we did by observing a baby anywhere between ten and eighteen months old. From then on, you can stand firm and not only walk steadily, but also run. To be able to do these feats, your backbone must not be too flexible like that of a baby. It must be firm so that it can support the upper body as well as the heaviest part, the head. I am sure you agree with that.

While we are awake, most of us either sit or walk. These days, because of the convenience of cars and other modes of transportation, we walk much less than, say, a hundred years ago. We typically walk anywhere between 3,000 and 5,000 steps per day. Now it is recommended to take 10,000 steps a day, which originated in Japan in the early 1960s. Japanese researchers led by Dr. Yoshiro Hatano determined that if they were to increase their steps to 10,000 steps per day, the result would be healthier, thinner people. So, you may walk typically anywhere from 3,000 to 5,000 steps per day for many years. When you were a baby, you

might have walked only a few steps, but you must have increased the number of daily steps, maybe into the thousands, quickly as you grew older. You were able to increase the number of steps because you learned to keep your body steady. In other words, you did not want to fall and hurt yourself.

Also, there was another big motivation. After learning how to walk steadily, you can start running. For a child, to be able to walk fast and run is very exciting, and some of you may remember the pleasure of running when you were a toddler. If you do not remember, then you can watch toddlers playing and see that they are all running around and smiling. They are full of energy and seem to be almost unstoppable. So, what do we do to steady our walk? We stiffen our body, especially the backbone, as it is much easier to control if it does not bend or sway. So, every time we stand up or even when we are sitting up, we learn to tighten the muscles and ligaments around the backbone to keep it stiff so that it will remain a solid stick or pole rather than a flexible one. I believe this conscious effort to keep the backbone steady, along with the natural process of body formation at a young age, results in an inflexible body.

If children either play a lot outside the house or happen to work in the field with their parents, they can keep a higher degree of flexibility. I suspect that people in the nineteenth century were more flexible than people in the twentieth century, including most readers. I believe the tendency is still growing more prominent since children of the twenty-first century tend to stay inside the house a lot longer, watching TV or playing computer games. Their body stiffens up more as they do not move it in a dynamic way as the children of past centuries did.

This is my theory, and I have not contacted any medical personnel to support my thinking, but I am pretty confident that I am right about this. If any of the readers are in the medical field or have expertise in kinesiology, I wish to hear from them.

Let us assume my hypothesis is correct and move on to the subject of how we can improve flexibility. Before we jump into the subject, you may say, "I do a lot of warm-ups and have even tried yoga (or whatever), but I am still inflexible. Can your method help?" My quick answer is yes, and I will share the basic concept of how to work on your body to make yourself more flexible. Please note that the object of this chapter is not to provide a how-to instruction, but rather to present the concept of this unique approach. To provide an adequate instruction, I would need to write a whole book on it. You can get personal instruction from me if you participate in one of the seminars I give around the world. You can also apply to be a student of my online dojo. I am selective with my students, and I am not taking too many more as it requires a lot of time and energy. I have three dedicated students around the world, and they are making excellent improvement in their *karatedo*.

OK, let us dive into the method now. Most calisthenics and warm-up exercises we do focus on the hip joints and the shoulder joints. You swing your arms around and rotate your hips or bend forward and backward, for instance. Well, these exercises are acceptable, and, to some extent, they are beneficial. They may give you a warm-up so that they will reduce injuries during a physical exercise such as karate. Unfortunately, those exercises will not give you the real relaxation of the body that is needed to bring fluid movements to your techniques. What they are missing is more attention to the backbone, which, for most people, is more solidified than necessary, meaning that the ligaments, or discs, between the vertebrae have been deactivated (or hindered) as flexible joints. In fact, this can and does happen to other joints, such as the ankles and the knees.

For instance, we Japanese used to sit in *seiza* (正座) in our house all day long as we did not have chairs there. So, our knees were accustomed to being fully bent and extended; therefore, doing the bunny hop did not cause us any knee injuries. Now the Japanese lifestyle has changed, and only a few sit in *seiza* in their house. I hear that the bunny hop exercise has been banned in Japanese elementary schools because so many students have complained of knee problems. It was a very popular and common exercise to strengthen our legs, not only in sports activities, but also in the general PE classes of our school days. Times have changed, indeed.

Let's go back to the backbone as this is the key area where we must focus. I would like the reader to look at the illustration of the backbone (right). It shows a rear and also a side view of the shape. What do you think? What does it look like? I practice several *kobudo* (古武道) weapons, one of them being the nine-section whip (*kyusetsukon* [九節棍]), and the backbone reminds me of that weapon (below left). I am sure most readers know that the backbone is curved into a shape that looks like an *S* from the side even though we have the incorrect notion that it is completely straight. I picked this illustration as it is shown with the skull on top, showing that the backbone supports and balances the heaviest part of our body, which is like balancing a baseball bat or a set of wine glasses on top of your hand. Anyway, what does it look like? Doesn't it sort of remind you of a snake (sorry if you happen to hate this animal)? I will not include an illustration of snake bones, but the idea of a snake becomes important when I explain exactly how we need to do the flexibility exercise a little later in this chapter. By observing the backbone illustration, I hope the reader gets a better feeling about how this bodily structure is constructed or assembled.

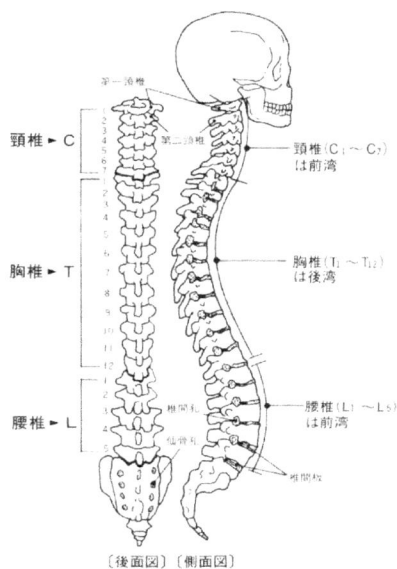

頸椎 ► C
胸椎 ► T
腰椎 ► L

頸椎(C₁～C₇)は前湾
胸椎(T₁～T₁₂)は後湾
腰椎(L₁～L₅)は前湾
椎間板

〔後面図〕〔側面図〕

Let's review again. There are seven vertebrae in the neck to support the head, twelve in the upper torso, and five in the lumbar area, totaling twenty-four movable bones. The top seven in the neck area are the easiest ones to move around but require the most care when moving about as you can easily sprain your neck because your head is so heavy. Moving too quickly or too suddenly can easily cause a sprain as you might have experienced in the past. The lumbar area may be a little more challenging but is still easy to move around. You can get a sprained back from bending forward and trying to pick up something very heavy.

The most challenging part is the twelve vertebrae between the neck and the lumbar portion. You will need to spend most of your time improving the flexibility of these vertebrae. Yes, each bone should be moved in all directions as we incorrectly believed that having a solid (rigid) backbone was good for walking. Well, once again, you may ask, "What's wrong with that?" Yes, balancing a baseball bat is easier than balancing stacked wine glasses. This is OK as long as you are not looking for fluid motion.

Let me give you an example from two world-class sprinters, Ben Johnson and Carl Lewis. Many readers will remember them as they competed in the same races, and, in fact, the hundred-meter final at the 1988 Summer Olympics was one of the most sensational sports stories of that year. Its dramatic outcome would rank as one of the most infamous sports stories of the century. Johnson won in 9.79 seconds, a new world record, while Lewis came in second at 9.92 seconds. Three days later, Johnson tested positive for steroids, which resulted in his disqualification, and Lewis moved up and was awarded the gold. Some readers may remember this as it was big news then.

I am not discussing his doping problem here but rather the way he built himself up with his body and the way he ran. Do you remember? He carried his upper body like a baseball bat or a Mack truck. He was fast as he had the leg and upper-body muscles to run fast, but his running was never beautiful. It almost looked funny and artificial. On the other hand, do you recall how Lewis ran? How would you describe it? You do not need to go to a *YouTube* video; just look at the two photos on these two pages. Johnson has huge thighs and upper-body muscles but looks cranky and even stiff. Lewis does not have huge thighs or big upper-body muscles, but he looks as though he is swimming or gliding through the air. This is what I call a fluid performance. Both of them were tops in the world in sprinting, but it makes that much of a difference in the body motion.

You must remember that Johnson was good only in the hundred-meter sprint and that his career was very short. Lewis won gold medals not only in the hundred-meter sprint but also in two-hundred-meter sprint and the long jump. In addition, he was the world champion for over seventeen years (1979–1996). He achieved excellent flexibility of the joints, including the backbone. He used his backbone to accelerate. If you want to see this, go check out his performance on *YouTube*. You will see how he does it. This could be done not only because he had strong legs, which I am sure he did, but more importantly because he could summon all the muscles of his body in harmony to achieve maximum results. This can be done only if all the joints are loose and movable and, in addition, if they are controllable and manageable.

Let me add one interesting point about these athletes as I clearly remember the specific reaction I had to them. Do you remember how you felt about their performances? I remember that, as we watched them on TV, we were impressed with the strong run by Johnson. He looked like a runaway two-ton truck coming down the street, and the way he

ran certainly was not beautiful. I do not know how you felt, but I, at least, didn't like his form. On the other hand, I loved how Lewis ran. I was almost enchanted with the smooth flow of his running style. So, when he lost to Johnson in the 1988 Olympics, we were disappointed as we wanted the "beautiful" runner to win. I am sure the Canadian people were happy.

When the doping was discovered a few days later, we did not feel sorry for Johnson. We instinctively loved something beautiful and not an "ugly" runner. Johnson's run was strong but not beautiful; thus, the people did not love it. Lewis' style was beautiful and looked natural. But, why did we feel his running style was beautiful and "right" when we did not feel this way about Johnson's?

Lewis made a big impression on us because—this is my personal theory— he did not solidify his upper body as Johnson did. This is only my assumption, but Johnson wanted to build a big and heavy upper body with two strong legs. Instead of focusing on muscle coordination, he probably did a lot of weight training to make himself strong. As a result, his upper body became like a big chunk of muscle. Lewis, on the other hand, was also in the long jump (lucky for him), for which he needed to bend his back and use his backbone power to jump; thus, he did not think of solidifying his body with a lot of weight training. Instead, he probably relied on his natural talent and trained to coordinate all the muscle groups in his body, leveraging the strong power generated by his backbone. This approach, I believe, kept his motion natural and also beautiful, which harmonized with our unconscious mind and resulted in pleasure and great admiration.

On a related note, I can also say something similar when I watch *kata* competitors (though this is not too often). Some competitors do their *kata* very quickly. I am impressed with their ability to move their arms and legs so fast. Yet, most of the time I am not moved as something is missing from their performance, and I am not talking about the tempo, rhythm, power, etc. I am not talking about the techniques either. I simply do not see the natural moves that flow from one technique to the next. The moves I see in most competitors are all rehearsed to simply move fast. No matter how fast they can move, I do not see the beauty in it even though we must not look for this in *kata*. But, I hope the reader understands what I am trying to say.

OK, let's go back to the use of the backbone for speed and creation of beautiful body motion. Maybe you are not totally convinced that the backbone makes that much of a difference. Let me show you another set of photos (below). Everyone knows that this is the cheetah, the fastest land animal, which can run as fast as 70 to 75 mph (112 to 120 km/h). I am sure you have seen a video of a cheetah running. What did you think? Isn't it beautiful how it can run? We already know it can run fast, but what impresses us more is its beauty.

Now pay attention to the backbone of the cheetah in these two photos. You can clearly see that it is contracting and expanding its backbone and using it to accelerate its running. If the vertebrae were stiff and unmovable, then the cheetah could not run like this. Carl Lewis was smooth and fluid in his running, but I'm sorry to say that his running form was no comparison to that of a cheetah. The latter exhibits an almost perfect motion of fluidity. I get very excited and emotional about this subject, so I could talk about the importance of the backbone for hours.

Now, you will probably say, "OK, I understand that it is important that the backbone be flexible, but how do I get my backbone loose?" As I stated earlier, teaching exercise in written form is extremely difficult and could be misunderstood. I must coach you in person to show you the fine details, but I will give you a couple of hints as it is not difficult or mysterious.

There are only three ways to move our body. One is twisting, or body rotation; another is side bending; and the last one is forward and backward bending. You practice the twisting motion in Tekki Shodan. Can you recognize which part? I wrote an article about this titled "Mystery of Tekki" last year. If you are interested, you can find it in one of the issues of *Classical Fighting Arts* (http://www.dragon-tsunami.org/Cfa/Pages/cfahome.htm).

For the sideways exercise, think of a snake (sorry again if you dislike this). You know how a snake moves, and you need to imitate the moves by bending or curving the backbone. It is not very easy to do this, and it will tell you how flexible or inflexible your backbone is. Once you get used to it, you can try it on the floor. You lie down on the floor and hold your hands behind your back. You need to move forward without using your legs by just swaying your body like a snake. Try it and you will find it extremely challenging.

For the last movement, bending forward and backward, I will not recommend imitating a cheetah or a dolphin. They move too quickly for our exercise. My hint is an inchworm or a Slinky. Yes, you can move your backbone in a similar manner, in other words, in an up-and-down motion, but it must be done slowly.

By the way, do you remember this toy, the Slinky? Maybe you have one in your house. It was invented in 1943 and, as of 2003, had sold more than 300 million units in that sixty-year span since its invention. It is also listed on the "Century of Toys List" by the U.S. Toy Industry Association.

This is such a simple toy, but why did it sell so well? I believe people were and are fascinated with its smooth and fluid motion. What do you think? Can we learn to move our backbone something like that or like an inchworm? If you

can, I guarantee you that your entire body motion will be smooth and fluid.

Conclusion

I present that the body muscles of most of us have been solidified or tightened up to an unnecessary (almost unhealthy) degree. I stated that we had learned this state when we were toddlers as we learned how to stand up and walk. Our body was very flexible then, and we did not know how to balance well. So, we overcompensated with our body, which was flexible then, by solidifying the ligaments of the backbone into one almost immovable unit. We kept this process with the backbone for so many years that we forgot how to loosen the vertebrae.

Having our core, the backbone, so rigid affects our entire body, almost all the muscles in our body being tightened up. This is why we find it difficult to relax our muscles. In other words, we tend to be tightened up almost all the time because the muscles are always being pulled or affected by the core.

Though we have a stressful society, the root cause of our inflexibility is not from the external world but rather from inside our body. I have concluded that our body muscles will remain tense most of the time unless we learn or regain flexibility of the core, the backbone. We may engage in yoga, tai chi, progressive muscle relaxation, etc., and we may feel good and somewhat relaxed during or right after exercise. But, this will only give temporary relief, and most of us will remain rigid and inflexible. This condition prevents us from achieving fluid body motions in our karate techniques.

Despite the fact that this trend is universal, there are some who have overcome this problem. We find a few experts in all fields, including sports, martial arts, and other arts, such as singing, dancing, and playing musical instruments. True experts seem to have learned to be fully relaxed and own a flexible body. I believe I have found a method to make all of us gain the true flexibility that only the experts enjoy.

What I am proposing in this chapter is that we need to train the joints, particularly those of the backbone, to relax and make them more movable. There are three directions of body movement, and our training must cover all of them. By the way, I close my eyes as I exercise my backbone or try to move the vertebrae. I try to open my "internal eyes" so that I can "see" what I am doing.

When the core is relaxed, mobility at the shoulders and the hip joints will be greater, which will result in a greater ability to relax those areas. Once we learn how to relax the body core and the major joints, it will be much easier to relax the rest of the body. In addition, by relaxing our body core, we will be able to manage our muscles and achieve fluid movements in our techniques.

What do you think? You may not believe in my method or even be convinced that it works, but isn't it worth giving it a chance and trying it once or twice? You have nothing to lose and everything to gain.

CHAPTER ELEVEN
第十一章

JIDOSHA DOJO (AUTOMOBILE STUDIO)
自動車道場は如何

Many agree that karate practice does not stay only in the dojo. Where do you practice outside the dojo? Some are lucky to have a big backyard or a large garage where they can do their practice. Some may go to a park or a school gym. What do you practice at those places? You can certainly practice *kata* and *kihon*. Can you practice *kumite*? Yes, only if you can find a partner. But, most of the time you will have to practice by yourself, so no *kumite*.

In this chapter, I propose the idea of training in your car, which includes *makiwara* and *kumite* practice. I call this *Jido-sha Dojo* ('Automobile Studio'). No, I am not proposing that you buy a bus or a big van to train inside. This idea does not include giving a loud *kiai* to the driver who is in the car next to you, pounding your fist against the steering wheel to toughen it up, or swinging your backfist at the passenger-side headrest, either. In fact, what I will share with you will not propose any techniques or movements that are not related to driving itself. What I am proposing is only your normal driving, but I will ask you to incorporate karate training into your driving, and I will describe what and how.

Many people drive to and from work daily. Some may spend more than an hour in the car each way. This means you spend more time driving than training in your dojo every week. Wouldn't you agree that it would be wonderful if you could add those hours to your karate training? You may say, "I sometimes think about *kata* or other karate techniques, but I cannot continue thinking about it because I am too busy driving." This is true, and it might be too dangerous if you were daydreaming or paying attention to something other than driving. What I will explain is completely different from what you are probably expecting. In fact, what I suggest will improve your driving performance if you follow it correctly.

There are several different training syllabi or menus. Let me share some of the main ones that you can include in your driving routine.

Menu #1: Distance Practice

One thing you must remember is that your car is an extension of yourself. Now, this is a very important concept, and I want the reader to fully understand this. So, I will spend some time on this subject first.

You already know that a meek person may feel braver when he is in a large truck than when he is in a smaller car. In his big truck, he will not be intimidated by a small car even if its driver may be a big and muscular guy. This is one example of the concept of a car's being an extension of oneself, but I am not talking about this emotional feeling that can be created by what kind of car one drives.

When I say, "Extension," what I am talking about is connected more to the physical aspect of your body. In fact, you must believe that the end of your body does not stop at the tip of your finger or at your skin, but rather goes out or extends further. It is true that there is a certain amount of space around you that you would consider a part of your "territory." I am sure you have encountered a situation in your life more than once where a person passes in front of you without saying, "Excuse me." I suspect you felt somewhat offended or invaded by this person or his act. If the distance between you and him had been a hundred meters or even ten meters, you would not have cared. But, you felt it was a very short distance, so you expected the common courtesy of "Excuse me."

Why did you feel that courtesy was needed? It is simply because we all have a space around us that we feel is our personal space or territory. In fact, there is a study called *proxemics*, the study of the cultural, behavioral, and sociological aspects of spatial distances between individuals. The amount of distance varies a lot by personal feelings and also by cultural custom. In some Asian countries, the distance tolerance is very high. For instance, the person behind you will stand very close to you when you are in line in Japan. I have been living in the U.S. for many years, so I often find myself feeling uncomfortable in the subway ticket line or the post office line when I visit Tokyo. Even within the same country, the distances vary if you are in a city, such as New York, or in a small village in a wide-open state, such as Idaho. Of course, the distance tolerance is much higher in New York, and a visitor from Idaho would probably feel very uncomfortable in a crowded New York City subway. If you are interested in learning more about proxemics, you may want to access to this site: http://proxemics.weebly.com/index.html.

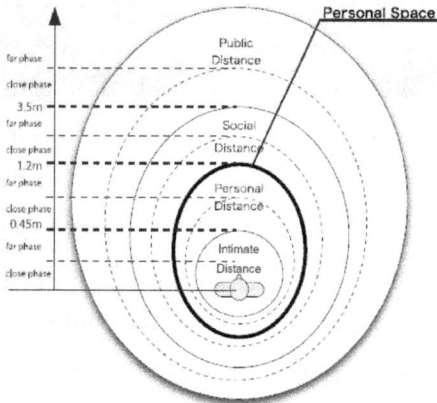

Modeling the spatial behaviour of virtual agents in groups for non-verbal communication in visual worlds by Hamid Laga et al. Tokyo Institue of Technology

So, there is a space you recognize as part of you or that you consider to be your space. What I will ask is that you go further with this feeling. If you drive a small car in your daily life, then when you have to drive a larger car, you feel uncomfortable, especially when you have to park or drive on a narrow road or bridge. You feel even more uncomfortable or insecure if you have to drive a big van or a truck. This is a good example of body extension when you drive. An experienced bus or truck driver has no problem even with parallel parking or driving over a narrow bridge. He can "extend" himself to the outside of his bus or truck and knows exactly how far he (or his bus or truck) can or cannot go. He has a greater body distance than we (small-car drivers) do. This is definitely a learned skill, and a professional truck driver must go to a special school for this. This ability to extend body distance can also apply to the use of a weapon, such as a sword, a *bo* (棒), or a nunchaku (ヌンチャク). I will not go into this subject here as we are focusing our discussion on automobile driving right now, but I am sure the reader can guess how it applies.

We also talk about a long-distance fighting method, which is characteristic of Shotokan karate, compared to a short-distance fighting method, which is used in arts such as Goju Ryu. I believe the training method I will share will help both fighting styles, but I think the benefit is greater for Shotokan practitioners as it will expand the territory or space that is controlled by you.

I will present two types of training here that you can use to train in your car. One is automobile *makiwara* training; the other one is automobile *kumite*.

In automobile *makiwara* training, I am not suggesting that you run into a post or make a *makiwara* out of an old tire. It is only a metaphor, and I am suggesting that you pay more attention when you park your car in your garage or in a public parking lot. Your training is to not hit the front or the side (particularly the passenger side) of your car on anything around you. This is totally opposite of *makiwara* training as you are not supposed to hit anything in automobile *makiwara* training, but it is still distance practice. You must be able to extend yourself to the outline of your car. The obstacles in your garage or other parked cars can be your "partners." If you are skilled at this training, your car will stay scratch free for many years. In addition, you will be an expert at parallel parking. Check your skill and see if you need more training or not.

In automobile *kumite*, I am not proposing that you bump your car against another or attack other cars or drivers. In fact, it is better called *automobile taisabaki* (体裁き) as you try to keep the correct distance from all the cars around you. The first thing you must do is stop being a tailgater if that is your habit. I will discuss this more in Menu #4, but having sufficient distance between you and the car in front of you is very important. It may be easier on a highway or a freeway, but it will take much more practice and close attention on a busy city street, and that is the best *kumite* situation for you.

In dojo *kumite*, you typically have only one opponent. You are lucky if your sensei puts you in multiple-opponent *kumite*, but I am sure you will not usually face more than two or three opponents. On the other hand, what you can do here is distance training with many opponents (cars) around you, not only with the ones in front of you, but also with the ones beside you and even behind you. I will talk more about rear training in Menu #3 as it requires a different technique. Here we will focus on the cars in front and to the side.

You will have training for at least three separate distances here. With the car in front of you, your training is to keep the same distance. If it slows down, check how soon you react to the difference in distance. The driver in the car in front of you may not pump the brake to alert you. Your training is to detect the difference in distance by visual observation. This visual check from a car that is running at even a moderate speed of thirty or forty miles per hour will help you with your visual judgment in real *kumite*. Training with the cars on your sides will require more than distance practice, so I will explain this further in Menu #2.

Menu #2: Practice Perceiving Other Drivers' Intentions

This is training to learn the concept that was presented by Musashi Miyamoto (宮本武蔵, c. 1584–1645) in his famous quote: "Perceive that which cannot be seen with the eye." Your training with the cars on your sides is to develop your alertness for a car that may turn in to yours by mistake or cut in front of you without warning. If this happens, you need to be ready to either swerve away or put on the brakes to avoid an accident. This is almost like train-ing to read the mind of the drivers in the cars around you. If you have a mind-set for this training, then you can develop a skill to detect movement by another driver and almost read his mind to know whether he is thinking of turning or not. A lot of times your car may be in the blind spot of another driver, and this is a dangerous moment. If you are alert, then you can avoid an accident. Certainly, you need to pay attention to the other cars that may get into your car's blind spots. You must not depend on the rearview mir-ror when you change lanes or turn corners. You must turn your head and verify with your own eyes that it is clear to the side you are turning in to.

You must also be alert to the car in front of you. There are three cases: (1) cars going the same direction as you, (2) cars coming toward you, and (3) cars waiting at an intersection to cross the street.

Let's look at case number 1, cars going the same direction as you. You must always expect that the driver in front may have a sudden need to brake hard and stop. If you have sufficient distance, this action will not bring you into a scary situation; rather, being ready all the time will give you a faster reaction, and you will not need to brake hard yourself. This (not braking hard) will decrease the possibility of getting hit by a car from behind. To avoid this type of accident, it is better to make several separate pumps on the brake to let the other driver know that you are putting the brakes on. I will go further regarding the driver behind you, but, here again, you must not assume that this driver is alert and is a safe distance away from you. Paying attention to the back is very important. Though you may not be the cause of the accident, who wants to be in an accident, regardless of who is at fault.

In the case of number 2, cars coming toward you, you also need to pay full attention as this driver may decide to turn and cross the street in front of you.

It is amazing, but sometimes the driver in that car does not see your car or may misjudge the distance and timing. You need to be ready for any sudden moves by a car that is approaching you. Do not assume the driver in that car will see you or will make a safe and proper judgment.

This can apply to case number 3, as well, which is when a car is either merging into your lane from another lane or is waiting at an intersection and may suddenly get into your lane or cross the street in front of you. The key point here is to never underestimate your opponent or situation.

All of these situations are taught at a driving school, but we easily forget. Paying attention all the time for all possibilities and being ready for them is the martial art mind. Driving a car is the perfect opportunity to train and develop this attitude or mind-set and, after training, hopefully this will turn into an ability to perform almost unconsciously.

Menu #3: Practice Watching Your Back

Even though it might not be your fault when you are hit from behind, no one wants to have an accident, so you must learn to keep a safe distance between you and the car that is behind you. If the car behind you likes to tailgate, the best option for you is to change lanes. If there is no other lane, then stop and let him pass you. This is common sense, but not too many people follow this advice. What some people do is step on the brake to scare the guy behind them. Sometimes it may work, but other times it irritates or angers the other driver and may develop into a more dangerous situation. So, I strongly advise you to not use a braking action toward your tailgating opponent.

There is another exercise you will want to do for your rear training. A rearview mirror becomes very important here. Of course, I am not referring to using it to put your lipstick on or fix your hair. This is to watch out for a police car. Most of the time you get caught by a police officer that was trailing behind you. By developing this ability, you will have less of a chance of receiving a traffic ticket, and your automobile insurance will not go sky high. Seriously, a karate expert must not receive any ticket, not just by observing the rearview mirror, but by observing all the traffic laws.

Menu #4: Practice Controlling Your Emotions

This training is a part of automobile *kumite*. When a careless or impolite driver cuts right in front of you, do not honk or get upset. What you need to do is let off your accelerator so that you will slow down and allow more space between your car and his. As the driver in front of you is either careless or impolite, he is not a safe driver. Pay more attention to this car and exercise Menu #2. When you are having a bad day, this small incident may upset you. Of course, you need to train your feelings so that you will not let them dictate your reactions. In addition, you need to work more on Menu #2 so that a surprise move by the car next to you will not happen. If you can detect the feeling that this car is getting into your lane, you will let off the accelerator a little and make a space in front of you.

There is another situation where you need to control your feelings. You either cut someone off by mistake or drive too safely (slowly) and get another driver angry. If you offend another driver by cutting him off by mistake, then the best thing to do is

signal your apology. Most of the time the other driver may be upset, but he will forgive you if you wave your hand and apologize. However, there may be a

driver who gets so upset that he feels he needs to show his anger by retaliat-
ing. This person may want to pass you quickly and cut you off. If this happens,
the best thing to do is to go more slowly and let this person pass you. The best
strategy is to keep a safe distance from and ignore this unhappy driver. There
are many unhappy and upset drivers who are looking around for an emotional
outlet. You do not want to get caught by a person like this. There is no reason
for you to be a target of this negative feeling, and you should not let this person
risk your safety as well as that of your loved ones.

This is very good training to keep yourself calm in a conflict situation.
Interestingly, people are more likely to become impolite or rude in situations
that are not face-to-face, such as a car incident. This seems to be truer among
males. If you happen to meet them in a supermarket or in a library, they may
offer to open the door for you or may say, "After you," and let you go first. The
lack of a face-to-face situation in traffic encourages people to be less polite or
considerate. This situation is probably less common among women. Whether
you are a man or a woman, avoid these impolite people and keep a good *maai*
from those who are looking for trouble.

Menu #5: Practice Driving with Minimum Brake Action

Now I will complete this
chapter with the most advanced
training menu for Jidosha Dojo.
The idea is simple and clear, but
doing it correctly and safely can
be very challenging. Driving with
minimum braking action is fairly easy on a freeway, where you
have little traffic. You can set your car on cruise control and just drive. However, once you are in a town or a city and have to drive on a city street, it is not

so easy. Why am I adding this as a menu? Is this something a retired person with a lot of time but not enough excitement wants? No, this menu will require a lot of mind work and discipline. One point to work on is distance perception involving other cars, traffic lights, and other traffic signs and obstacles. Another is time perception, when to step on the brake and when to release it. You will also have to fight against your desire to speed up sometimes, but you will need to make a judgment if that is required or advisable.

In the end, your driving will improve, and your car will perform very smoothly. The passengers in your car will not feel any jerky or quick-stopping movements. They will also feel very safe as your car just glides through the traffic like a flying carpet. It is true that some of the drivers behind you may not like your speed or the way you are driving. Your driving style may be different and unusual. They may honk or yell at you. I advise you to let them pass you quickly so you can keep smiling.

There are, of course, other syllabi you can incorporate in Jidosha Dojo training, such as breathing, stretching, reaction, etc. But, if you get good at the five exercises I listed here, your car performance will change, and you will drive differently. It will certainly be much safer. You will most likely avoid receiving any traffic tickets. You will have much less of a chance of getting involved in a car accident. Initially, you may find it challenging, but once you get used to it or master the art, you will enjoy your driving much, much more. In addition, you will realize that Jidosha Dojo training will help you with your karate in both the physical and the mental aspect.

One thing I can confidently say is that what I am proposing here will increase the safety of your driving experience even if it does not help you with your karate. Another thing I want to add is a controversial statement. If you claim that you are a karate or martial arts expert, then you must be able to prove this by your driving history. A diploma that may show a high rank is not good enough for a true qualification. One qualification a karate expert must

produce is a clean traffic history and record since the time he began to call himself a karate expert. I consider what I am stating here to be very fair. However,
I wonder how many karate experts can share their driving history to satisfy
this qualification.

Whether you wish to try out my training ideas or not, Jidosha Dojo is your
choice, and I do not expect that all readers will do it. But, think of your life
without any accidents or traffic tickets. Isn't it worth giving it a try even for a
short period of time to see if it will make any difference?

CHAPTER TWELVE
第十二章

THE ART OF PERFECT SHAVING
芸術的な髭の剃り方とは如何に

In this chapter, I will discuss the art of shaving. I am not joking about the art part of this activity. Most men need to engage in it daily. Yes, I am very serious that there is an art to the handling of a razor. If you happen to use an electric razor, then this may not apply as well as with a regular safety razor. One high-ranking Western sensei commented after he heard about my idea, saying that "shaving is only shaving, and there is no art in it." I am afraid he does not understand the depth of the art that could extend to small actions such as shaving.

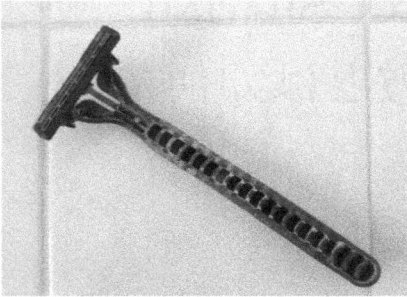

Here is a photo of my razor (left). It is a popular brand and an inexpensive two-blade razor. I do not know how long you can keep using the same razor, but a friend of mine told me his razor barely lasts one month before he tosses it. Believe it or not, mine lasts for more than two years (yes, *years*), and I suspect that is probably longer than the time of most, if not all, readers. The razor shown here is more than a year old now and is a little dirty, but it will continue to give me a nice shave for at least one more year. My beard is stiff and coarse, so my razor gets normal use. I use the same razor for a long time, certainly not because I am stingy. I do throw my razor away but only when it stops giving me a good shave. Any razor can last that long if you use it correctly. Needless to say, I am not sharing the art of perfect shaving so that you can save money. I am sure that may not motivate you enough to read this chapter.

Then, why am I doing this? Let me tell you that the techniques that are used in a perfect shave are connected to the core concepts and techniques of the martial arts, certainly including karate. Now, I hope this statement will capture your attention. My claim may be difficult for some to believe right now, so I ask that you continue to read till the end of this chapter. At the end, you can decide if what I am telling you makes sense or if it is a bunch of BS.

Obviously, the razor I have is something I bought at a common drug store, and it must be very similar to the ones you use. So, the difference is not the tool itself; rather, it is the method or the technique that is different. The first secret to perfect shaving rests in how you hold the razor.

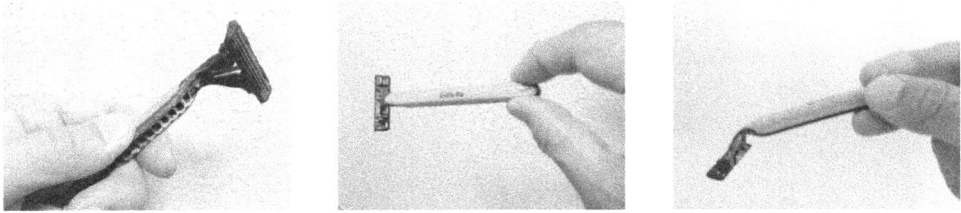

| 1 | 2 | 3 |

Picture 1 shows a standard holding method, which I suspect is similar to how you hold yours. The way I hold my razor is shown in Picture 2 (the two-finger method). I hold the end of the handle with just my thumb and index finger. This is an expert holding method, and I know it will be very difficult for you to get any shaving done with this method. To start the perfect shaving lesson, I recommend that you hold the razor as depicted in Picture 3 (the three-finger method), where you hold the end of the handle with your thumb and middle finger and put light pressure on the back of the handle with your index finger. Once you get used to this method of holding the razor, believe it or not, you will have better control of the razor with this method.

Before we go into the actual technique of shaving, let us look at other arts and physical activities that are both Japanese and non-Japanese. Here I wish to elaborate on the correlation between the holding techniques of the razor and those of other tools.

The first one is the Japanese writing brush (*mohitsu* [毛筆]). After looking at some artistic Chinese writing, I am sure you will agree that you see an art form when you look at the brushed writing with its beautiful strokes (see example on the following page).

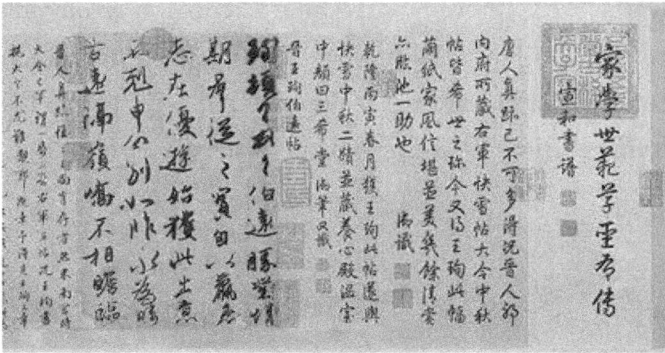

So, how do you hold a brush? One standard holding method is shown in Picture A. You keep the brush vertical as you write the characters. The holding method here is similar to how you hold a pen or a pencil, so you should not be surprised by this. However, when you get into more artistic or sophisticated writing, an artist may hold the brush in the way shown in Picture B. Isn't this similar to the holding method that I suggested for the razor earlier? Interesting, isn't it?

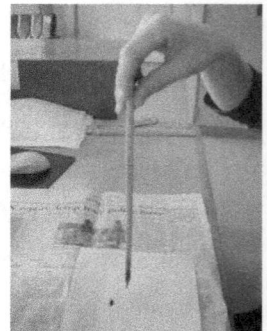

A   B

Many readers probably like Japanese food, such as sushi and tempura, and may frequent Japanese restaurants. There you have the option to eat with a knife and fork or a pair of chopsticks (*hashi* [箸], or *ohashi* [御箸]).

The degree of skillfulness with chopsticks seems to indicate how much a person likes Japanese food. If you are a first-time visitor, you may have to resort to a crude method (Picture C on next page) so you can eat (survival mode,

I guess). Eventually, you will develop the skill of holding a pair of *ohashi* in an acceptable manner (Picture D). Take a look at the third photo (Picture E). This is a photo of a Japanese tempura chef, a professional in the art of Japanese food. Notice that he holds the very top part of the chopsticks.

 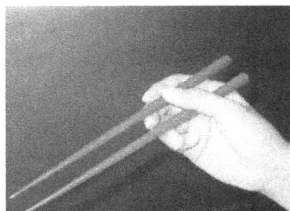 

C D E

We just saw the way to hold a brush, and here is the way to hold a pair of chopsticks. Wouldn't you agree that to do a fine job with a small tool, it is better to hold it at the end and work it from there? I hope so, but it is OK if you are still not fully convinced. You can experiment with a pair of chopsticks, a brush, or a razor. They are all cheap and very common, so the experiments are easy to do.

While you are experimenting with these small tools, I want to move on to other tools that are somewhat larger and heavier. As I am trying to tie this subject to the martial arts, let's look at the Japanese sword, the katana.

Now, I confess that I have never learned iaido (居合道) or kenjutsu (剣術). Thus, I am not an expert in this matter. However, I have trained with *kobudo* weapons, such as the *sai*, nunchaku, *tonfa*, etc.; thus, I know that the fundamental method of holding a weapon is similar. Here is a photo showing 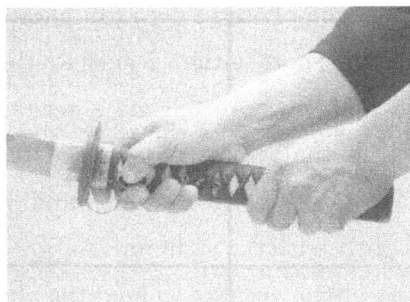 how to hold a sword. Notice the front hand. Pay very close attention to the thumb and the index finger. As you can see, they are not holding tightly, which is a key point.

By the way, do you remember when you first learned how to make a fist when you joined a karate club? If the instructor taught you correctly, he must have told you to start bending the little finger tightly first, then the ring finger, then middle finger (see below). After those three fingers are held tightly, you bend the index finger last and then complete the fist by lightly placing the thumb over the index finger.

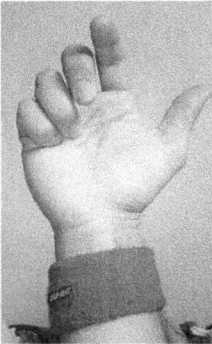

I hope the instructor told you to squeeze the little finger and the ring finger tightly, but not so tightly with the middle finger, and even more loosely with the index finger and the thumb. Of course, this is the fist you make in *kamae* or *yoi*. When you punch an opponent or a *makiwara*, you tighten all the fingers but only at the point of impact, after which the fist will be held loosely again. The concept here should be similar to, or the same as, when you handle a sword. Hold the sword tightly with the little finger and the ring finger. The middle finger is there to give support. The index finger and the thumb are used for managing or handling the sword. If you are a kenjutsu or iaido expert, and if my understanding of holding a sword is incorrect, please let me know. However, I assume I am correct as that is the way it is in my *kobudo* training.

I want to bring up another interesting fact with a very popular sport called *golf*. The photo below right shows how to hold a golf club. I am not an expert in this sport, either. I suspect that some readers may be very experienced in it, and they can tell me if what I am saying here is correct or not. I understand that you are supposed to hold the club tightly with the left hand but not as tightly with the right one. As you can see in the photo, you are to hold the club ever so gently with the right hand. Take note that the thumb and index finger are positioned very similarly to the right hand when hold-

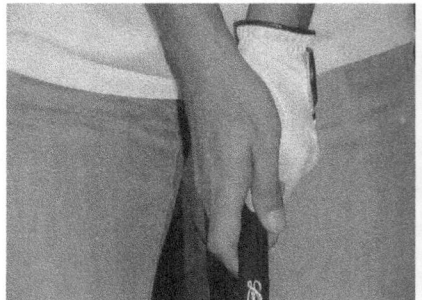

ing a sword (photo shown previously). Is this a coincidence? No, I don't think so. Thought the motion of the arms is quite different between these two arts—I am daring to call golf an *art* as it can be—the basic concept of holding the tools, the sword and the club, is the same. This suggests that the art of swinging a long object in a precise manner requires the same physical positioning and control.

I believe the basic concept of holding other long objects, such as a cue stick (billiards) or a bow for a violin or cello, must be the same or similar as the mechanism of our body is the same, no matter what activities we may do (see the photo to the

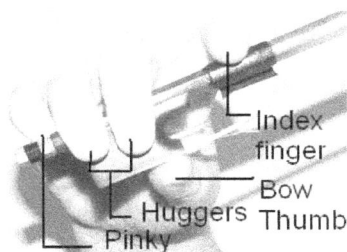

right). Here the little finger is not used much to hold the bow as it is not heavy. I suspect it is used more for balance and control of the bow. If you are a violin or cello player, maybe you can send me your comments as to whether my understanding is correct or incorrect.

As swinging a golf club is totally different from handling a sword, let me bring up another art, chopping or cutting wood. I believe this will be an excellent comparison as its mechanism quite resembles that of sword cutting. Wood cutting is not very popular in the warmer regions of the U.S., such as California, but I understand that it is a very popular activity and an important part of normal life in colder countries, such as Canada, Norway, or Sweden. I would love to hear feedback from those who chop wood regularly after you read this chapter.

So, here is the tool, an ax (right). The weight distribution is different, but its average weight is closer to that of a real sword than the *bokken* (wooden sword) or the *shinai* (bamboo sword) used in kendo. A while ago, I thought it might be interesting to investigate whether there was

any relation between this activity and kenjutsu, the art of the Japanese sword. So, here is what I found. The wood cutting I am discussing here is not for cutting down trees but for chopping a large piece of wood into smaller pieces for wood-burning purposes.

After identifying the tool, we need to discuss how to hold the tool, which is a part of the art, and I have mentioned this before. It is important as holding the tool correctly will help you get the best, or should I say, the most efficient cut. What do I mean by "best" and "most efficient" cut? This means you hit the center of the piece of wood every time and cut it in one strike. Of course, you will not miss one chop as that would be a waste of your energy. "Best" also means that you will not get tired even if you continue to cut wood all day long. Moreover, efficient activity does not give you a sore back, shoulders, legs, or arms. If you can do this, then you can say that you raised this activity to the level of an art form, and it will no longer be a chore but rather something you enjoy doing.

OK, so you understand the objective. Let's go back to holding the ax. Some people hold it above the shoulder as in the photo shown above left. The stance shown in the photo to the right is called *hasso no kamae* (八双の構え), which is one of the main *kamae* in kenjutsu. So, you may want to believe that holding an ax in a similar way is OK. I am sorry, but I do not believe that is the case for chopping wood.

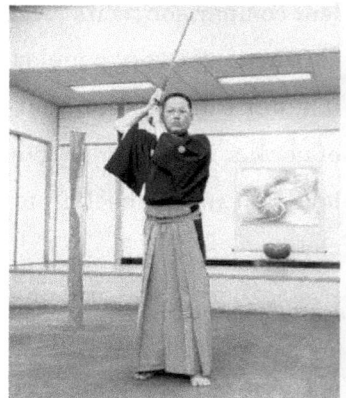

It is very obvious when you think of how you cut the opponent with a sword. The typical sword-cutting line is diagonal. Why? Obviously, it is better to cut the opponent's neck than to hit him right on top of the head. So, in most *tameshigiri* (試し切り, 'test cutting'), you see a bamboo stick or a roll of bound straw positioned in a vertical manner, and the demonstrator cuts it diagonally (photo below left). But, do they not have *tameshigiri* with the sword cutting straight down? Yes, in fact, at one of the shrines in Japan, Nakamura Jinja (中村神社), a demonstrator cuts a cinder block (photo below right).

OK, if you cut it straight down, how do you hold the sword? It doesn't take a rocket scientist to figure out that you hold it straight up above your head. In one of the famous kenjutsu styles, Jigen Ryu (示現流), which is popular in Kyushu, they practice swinging the sword by striking a log just as we punch a *makiwara*. The only difference is that the log is held horizontally (illustration below right), while our *makiwara* is vertical as you know. (Note: this kenjutsu training method is believed to be the origin of the *makiwara*, which was invented on Okinawa.)

Now notice the position of the sword in the drawing on the right as it is important, and I wish to go further on this particular subject. If this is the *kamae* of kenjutsu, am I suggesting that we should hold an ax in the same way? Yes, that is exactly what I am proposing. I know it is a daring proposal as I am not a sword expert and have never studied kenjutsu in my life. In addition, my experience with cutting wood is very limited. Then, how can a person like me with an amateur background in these

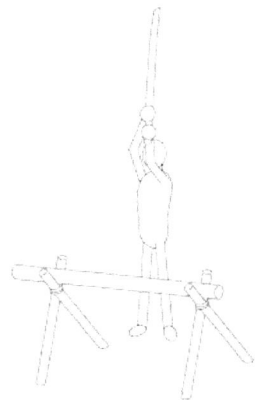

fields propose something like this?

Am I just guessing or BSing? I certainly hope not. I am quite confident about this and am explaining how it should be performed from the understanding of kinesiology as well as the *budo* requirement that demands the most effective body movements. What do I mean by "the most effective body movements"? This simply means that a technique must not only be fast, powerful, and accurate but also the most energy efficient. In other words, swinging a sword with only brute force is not considered a *budo* approved movement. The beauty or the artistic part of kenjutsu comes from efficient body movement that utilizes the minimum amount of muscle power leveraged by the help of gravity and the balance/off-balance mechanism. I have already written an article on the balance/off-balance mechanism under the title of "Unstable Balance," so I will not go into this area at this time.

Let us look at some examples of inefficient or poor wood-cutting techniques. First, look at the photo on the right and compare it to Picture J on page 190, which is how a Jigen Ryu sword practitioner would hold a sword. Very similar, isn't it? Let's examine this *kamae*. The stance is good as the feet are placed at about the distance of a *kiba dachi*. However, the position of the ax is not the most desirable as it is not held straight up, and the handle is leaning backward. Why is this bad? From this position, he needs to lift the ax to the highest level before he can bring it down to the wood, which is an unnecessary move. He needs to use the muscles of the shoulders, back, arms, and all other related body parts. Therefore, he needs to hold the ax upright as in the kenjutsu drawing shown earlier. This is a very accurate drawing as it shows the man holding his sword vertically. The sword itself is quite heavy despite the fact that it is not top-heavy like an ax. Holding it vertically like this is most efficient.

F   G   H

If you look at Picture F above, you will quickly realize why this *kamae* is not in accordance with the *budo* method. You can easily guess that this person will run out of energy after thirty minutes of wood chopping. In addition, he will probably wake up the next morning with soreness in his shoulders, arms, and back.

OK, what is wrong with the guy in Picture G? It is obvious, as you can guess, that he will have a sore back. As he chops, he leans his upper body forward. He is, in fact, too far away from the piece of wood. He will use a lot of his arm, shoulder, and back muscles to bring the ax down. After one hour of this exercise, he will have a bad pain in his lower back and possibly in his right shoulder when he gets up the very next morning.

Let's look at Picture H. How is she doing? She is doing much better, isn't she? I assume that she had her legs stretched when in her *kamae* and that she brought the ax down using its weight, going into a *shiko dachi* as the ax hit the wood. When compared to the man in Picture G, her right arm is much closer to her body (good point #1), and her hands are closer to each other (good point #2). Of course, I do not know if she held the ax straight up when in her *kamae*, but her chopping action is much more effective and energy efficient.

If she were not bending her back so much, I would rate her wood-chopping art at an expert level. If she continues chopping all day, she will have pain in her lower back the next day. In addition, her feet are pointing outward (*shiko dachi*), which means that the falling energy will dissipate in other directions instead of being focused on the target, the piece of wood. Apparently, she is not a Shotokan practitioner, so, unfortunately, she does not know the benefit of the *kiba dachi*.

Let me show you some photos that, I believe, demonstrate expert wood chopping.

I

J

In the photos above (Pictures I and J), you can see an excellent *kamae* with a *naihanchi* stance (a bit shorter than a *kiba dachi*). The knees are slightly squeezed inward, and the ax handle seems to be held up in a very vertical position. The hands are held with some distance, but I assume she will bring them closer as she drops the ax down. This is a black-belt level *kamae*.

Yes, she will almost literally drop the ax as she will not use too much of her arm and shoulder muscles when she chops the piece of wood. In other words, what she will do is just let the ax fall toward the piece of wood. During this process, she will use her hands and arms only to guide the ax so that it will hit the piece of wood accurately.

The photo to the left shows exactly how you want to drive the ax through the wood by bending your knees deeply as you can see. You will notice that the wood cutter's stance looks like an excellent *kiba dachi* or *shiko dachi*. You will also notice that

his back is not bent forward too much and that his hands are held closely together. I can assume he just cut the wood at an expert level by leveraging the
gravity of the ax. As a result, he used the minimum amount of his strength and
energy. Using this method, he could probably cut wood all day long without
ever getting tired, and he will not have any back or shoulder pain the next
morning (black-belt level).

When you become a real expert, you can get down to the depth shown in the photo on the right and use the full gravity of the ax as well as your own body weight with a *zanshin* feeling. Look how straight his back is. He will not have any backaches afterward for sure. He can continue to  chop all day long without getting tired. Of course, you must have strong legs to perform at this expert level, but I am sure that most readers who are *karateka* can develop their technique to a black-belt level pretty quickly.

What do you think of this method? If you regularly cut wood, I would like
you to try this and get back to me if this method made any difference in your
activity.

The *budo* method of efficient movement can be applied to almost all bodily
functions in our daily life. I suggest that you reevaluate how you walk, sit, drive
(see Chapter 11: "Jidosha Dojo"), play golf, play any musical instrument, etc.,
and see if your movements are in accordance with the *budo* method. Wouldn't
you agree that most of the time we can tell if a driver is experienced or is a
student driver by looking at the way he sits and holds the steering wheel?

We have digressed a lot, so let's go back to the art of perfect shaving. You
have read that the method of holding the tool is important. You have seen the
pictures of how a razor can or should be held, but you wonder if this is the end
of the technique. No, I have not covered the actual technique of perfect shaving

yet. Holding the razor correctly is only
the beginning.

Finally, let me explain the shaving method. Not to disappoint you, but
it is quite simple. You will remember
that you need to hold your razor very
lightly with two or three fingers. Now, here is the secret. You go over your face
with it as if you were petting your face with a feather. It almost sounds like a
commercial. In fact, there is a company with that very name that produces razor blades for the older type of safety razor (above). Seeing that *Feather* is the
company name, I suspect that the founder of that company must have known
how to shave correctly.

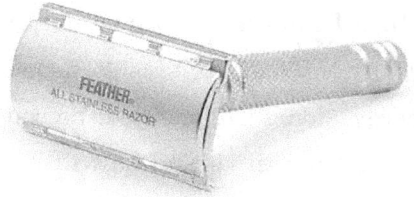

However, you may complain that you can't shave your beard well if you do
it as I explained. That is true, but that is exactly what is expected. The idea
here is not to chop the beard from the root with one stroke. You are expected to
go over the surface of the face many times and to cut the beard little by little
in a gradual manner.

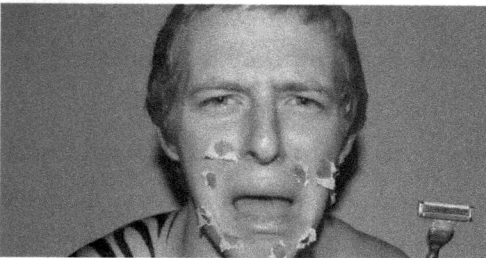

Why is this necessary? Both
shaving methods, crude and artful,
will give you a shave, but the artful
method will not cut your face. After
shaving, have you ever had to put
pieces of tissue on your face to stop
the bleeding? I suspect you have. Now, is this a big deal? It should be if you
claim to be a martial artist.

I do not know about you, but I consider it to be a part of self-defense. Maybe
my definition of *self-defense* is much broader than yours, but, for me, it includes preventing or avoiding all accidents, from a simple shaving cut to a
serious car accident (see Chapter 9: "What Is 'Complete' Self-Defense?"). I also
include avoiding sickness and illness as a part of my self-defense objectives.

From this perspective, a perfect shave will not draw blood, and, moreover, it will not give you a skin irritation or a rash afterward. If you shave close to your skin with much force, the blade will shave not only your beard but also your skin. Even if you do not shave off your skin, the roots of your beard will be pulled out by the shaving action, and that causes irritation as the skin on your face is very sensitive. You can check this by applying some aftershave to your face. If it burns the skin on your face, then you shaved too hard.

Even if you do not agree on the self-defense part, just think of the consequences of having cuts and rashes on your face daily. I certainly think that will age your face skin much faster. I guarantee that a perfect shave will help you stay looking young and healthy. It is up to you to decide if this benefit is good enough to motivate you to learn the art of perfect shaving.

CHAPTER THIRTEEN
第十三章

MASTER ASAI'S HIP POSITION MYSTERY
浅井先生、腰の位置の謎

When I posted a photo of Master Asai (left) on Facebook, someone commented that Master Asai's butt was sticking out. The same person commented that Master Kase, of France (JKA), also had the same posture. I cannot write about Master Kase as I know almost nothing about him and his karate. But, I believe I can present my theory on Master Asai. I will, hopefully, be able to shed some light on why he is standing that way. I believe there is a good explanation for his posture. I have studied Asai karate for over ten years and had a very close training relationship with him for the last few years of his life, between 2002 and 2006, the year he passed.

Before I go into my theory, I would like to take this opportunity to introduce Tetsuhiko Asai. Of course, most readers already know who Master Asai was. He was a world-renowned Shotokan master who traveled around the world and awed everyone with his almost magical techniques. I am well aware of his abilities, but I want to speak about Master Asai because I have a compelling reason. This will also explain why I started my organization, ASAI. Some people have accused me of taking advantage of his fame by using his name to name my organization. On the surface, indeed, it does appear so. Hopefully, by reading my explanation, the reader will understand that I have a much deeper motivation to keep his name and his karate alive.

Let me explain. Without any exaggeration, he saved my karate and, in essence, my karate life (I will explain the details later). I owe him so much, and now it is my turn to pay it back to the karate world since I cannot do so to him. It became my conviction to spread and share the karate I learned from Master Asai. As long as I live, I do not want anyone to forget about Master Asai. I want the name of Asai to be remembered. This is the exact reason why I created the organization ASAI (Asai Shotokan Association International). We are not an

organization that just happened to pick up a famous
name or be part of a fad. We are an organization that
intends to do the following:

- Give everyone access to the Asai Karate System
- Provide a home for karate ronin
- Make *dan* examinations available to all organizations and styles
- Unite all karate practitioners, regardless of organizational differences
- Improve the karate skills of all members
- Preserve the discipline of the *Dojo Kun*
- Pass the legacy of Master Asai on to the next generation

Let's look at the history of Master Asai from his birth to his last day. I could write something from my memory, but I think it is more accurate and complete to quote from the *Wikipedia* article about him (http://en.wikipedia.org/wiki/Tetsuhiko_Asai).

Here is a direct quote from the *Wikipedia* page:

Early life

Asai was born on June 7, 1935, in Ehime Prefecture (on the island of Shikoku), Japan. He was the eldest of seven children. As a boy, he trained in sumo. In addition, his father (a policeman) taught him judo, kendo, and sojutsu. When he was 12 years old, he witnessed a fight between a boxer and a *karateka* (practitioner of karate); the karate combatant was able to disable his opponent with a kick, and Asai was impressed.

Karate career

In 1958, Asai graduated from Takushoku University, where he had trained in karate under Gichin Funakoshi, Masatoshi Nakayama, and Teruyuki Okazaki.

He trained hard and was allowed to sleep in the karate dormitory. At Nakayama's recommendation, he entered the JKA instructor training program and graduated from the course three years later. Asai won the JKA championship in *kumite* (sparring) in 1961, and in *kata* (patterns) in 1963. He was overall JKA champion in 1961, having come in first in *kumite* and second in *kata* that year. Asai became the first instructor to introduce karate to Taiwan. Through the second half of the 1960s, he taught karate in Hawaii for five years, with his students including Kenneth Funakoshi (a fourth cousin to Gichin Funakoshi).

Over the years, Asai advanced within the JKA, and was appointed as Technical Director. Following Nakayama's death, the JKA experienced political troubles and divided; Asai and colleagues (including Keigo Abe and Mikio Yahara) formed one group, while Nakahara Nobuyuki and colleagues formed another group—which in 1999 was officially recognized as the JKA. In 2000, he founded the International Japan Martial Arts Karate Asai-ryu and the Japan Karate Shoto-Renmei. Apart from the ranking of 9th *dan* in Shotokan karate, he also held the ranks of 3rd *dan* in jodo, 2nd *dan* in judo, 2nd *dan* in jukendo, and 2nd *dan* in kendo.

Later life

Reflecting on relations between JKA instructors who had graduated from Takushoku University, Asai said, "We all pretty much get on nowadays, contrary to our official stances and federations. In saying that, some of us don't, but isn't that life? ... I am happy to say that most of the deep rooted rivalry has gone amongst my peers. I think that the passing of Mr. Enoeda, Mr. Kase, Mr. Tabata and Mr. Shoji and so forth has brought many of us back to reality. Obviously this is not limited to Takushoku University; it is all about us international karate pioneers getting very old."

Asai's health deteriorated with age, and he underwent liver surgery on February 10, 2006. He died at 2:50 PM on August 15, 2006, leaving behind his wife, Keiko Asai, and their daughter, Hoshimi Asai. More than 2,000 people attended his funeral,

which was held on September 1, 2006, at Gokokuji Temple in Tokyo. Asai received the rank of 10th *dan* posthumously from the JKS, and was succeeded as President of the IJKA by his widow. Since that time, IJKA in Europe has apparently separated from K. Asai's IJKA. In 2013, Asai Shotokan Association International (ASAI) was formed by a former student of Asai, Kousaku Yokota, to propagate Asai's style of Shotokan.

In the past, I have written about how Master Asai saved my karate life, but many readers may have not read it yet, so I would like to share my short explanation here.

In the mid nineties, as I was approaching fifty years old, I was a *godan* and a lifetime member of the JKA, having practiced Shotokan karate for more than thirty years. At that time, I keenly felt that I had reached a plateau with my karate training and could not find any challenge or pleasure in further training. I visited different sensei and went to seminars given by masters such as Hirokazu Kanazawa and Masahiko Tanaka (田中昌彦, 1941–), but none of them could inspire me. As a result, I decided to retire from karate in 1997. This was a big move as I had always believed karate was part of my life. But, I decided to do so because I could no longer find a way to improve myself. So, I decided to study ki and hoped I could find a solution in this art.

I found a job in Tokyo, where I lived for two and a half years. During this period, I did not wear my *gi*, not even once. I entered a famous ki school called Nishino Ryu Kokyuho Dojo (西野流呼吸法道場) in Shibuya. To make a long story short, I could not find my answer in ki training.

I came back to California in 2000 and decided to teach karate in San Jose. At that time, I had already given up on improving my own karate. In 2001, Asai Sensei was giving a seminar in the area, and I participated. Of course,

I knew Asai Sensei from my JKA time and had met him several times in the past. I had also witnessed, with my own eyes, the impressive demonstration he gave at the JKA's All Japan Championship (1981 and 1982). But, until I participated in this seminar in 2001, I only considered him to be one of Shotokan's famous instructors and nothing more.

This seminar event happened five years before his passing, so he was in his mid sixties. Upon observing his techniques and moves very closely, I was simply dumbfounded by his agility, flexibility, and speed. I knew immediately that he was the answer to my question of how I could improve my karate when I was in my sixties.

It took me a year before I finally left the JKA and became a follower of Master Asai. My close association with Master Asai began only five years before he left us all too soon. He knew so much, and I just did not have enough time or occasions to ask all the questions I had. I could never claim that I learned all of his techniques. He knew more than a hundred *kata*, and I have only learned twenty-five Asai *kata*. Despite this, I feel that I learned enough to share this knowledge and these techniques with all Shotokan practitioners, especially the advanced (in terms of both technique and age) *karateka*.

His karate was different, and my karate became different from the standard Shotokan karate. It is different because I feel my moves are more natural and smoother. I guess I would have to ask the reader to watch me either in person or via video performance to see if he thinks that this is true. I am convinced that the benefits are great for *karateka* of all styles and ages. I could never replace or duplicate all of Asai Sensei's techniques, but it is my lifetime mission to share what I know and do what I can do. This year (2014) I am sixty-seven years old, and I plan to do this for at least the next thirty-three years (God willing), so I will be around and so will ASAI.

OK, that is enough about my karate life. If you know Master Asai's karate, you will agree that his karate was not only great; it was different. You can see him in action and right away you will see definite differences. His moves and

techniques are smoother and more circular compared to the linear and somewhat rigid techniques that many Shotokan practitioners exhibit. You may ask
why his karate was so different. This
is quite difficult to explain. How did he
develop his karate? The answer to this
question will give you a hint as to the original question regarding the position
of his butt.

He became Technical Director of the JKA in the eighties, but before that
time, there was a very important stage of his karate life, specifically between
1965 and 1975. The JKA had dispatched him overseas to teach karate, starting
in Hawaii. After completing his assignment in Hawaii, he went to Taiwan in
the late sixties. I heard that Master Asai had some exposure to other styles of
karate and even to some kung fu styles while he was in Hawaii. He was always
looking for something new to try and to learn, so it is easy to guess that the
diversified martial arts found on the islands of Hawaii would have given him
many opportunities.

However, when he was sent to Taiwan, he got into some intensive training
in White Crane (*báihèchuán* [白鶴拳]), a style of kung fu. He became a close
friend of a kung fu expert, Master Chen, whose sister would eventually become
his wife. Master Asai was already a karate expert, so Master Chen did not
treat him like a student but rather like a martial arts partner. I heard from his
widow that they exchanged techniques all the time whenever they met. Master Chen would show a new or interesting technique one day, and Master Asai
would master that technique almost instantaneously, which impressed Master
Chen greatly. Obviously, he received a lot of influence from White Crane kung
fu.

OK, so you may be asking, "What has this got to do with Asai Sensei's
butt?" I believe there is a strong relationship here, so let me share this new

idea with you.

I found something interesting as I did research into the martial arts of Japan and China. What I found is that there is a difference between the two categories in the positioning of the pelvis. In other words, among the Japanese martial arts, the correct pelvis position is for it to be tucked in, that is, with the tailbone pointing downward. On the other hand, in the Chinese martial arts, the pelvis is positioned outward or pushed out. The visible difference is minor, but if you examine closely, you can see it.

Let's look at some photos of judo, kendo, and iaido.

What do you think? Can you see the positioning of the pelvis? Especially in the judo photo (above left), we can see the tucked-in pelvis position. By the way, this photo (above left) is one of the rare historical ones of Jigoro Kano (嘉納治五郎, 1860–1938 [person on right]), founder of Kodokan Judo (講道館柔道), taken early in the twentieth century.

Not convinced? Look at the sumo photo to the right. Even though this sumo wrestler is big and "fat," his pelvis down and tucked in. I put the word *fat* in quotation marks because the fat content of many sumo wrestlers is much lower than we think, and they

are not medically fat. Regardless of this point, I hope you can see the position of the pelvis better as he is without any clothing except for his *mawashi* (回し).

Next, let's look at some photos of the Chinese martial arts and see if we can detect any differences. Here are three typical kung fu photos that show a horse stance or another similar stance.

Upon checking the positioning of the pelvis of these female performers, would you agree that all three are sticking their pelvis outward and do not have it tucked in? Of course, I showed you only a few photos, so you may not see the clear differences between the Japanese arts and the Chinese arts. However, the difference is common knowledge among senior martial artists in Japan. I am afraid not enough research has been done yet to conclude why there is a difference in the basic concept of the positioning of the pelvis between the two groups.

Now, what I dare to present here is my hypothesis for the difference. The foundation of the Japanese martial arts is kenjutsu, fencing. Unlike some of the lightweight kung fu swords, a Japanese katana is quite heavy. If you happen to practice iaido, you know what I am talking about. Obviously, it would be very difficult to swing it around quickly, let alone jump with it. Therefore, the fighting style of the samurai had almost no moving around. The posture was very straight with the legs almost fully extended and the backbone straight to support the weight of the sword. You may have seen this in a Japanese samurai movie in which two samurai face each other in a duel, almost motionless until the decisive attack at the end. In this situation, it makes sense to keep the pelvis tucked in to support the body weight and assist with forward movement (remember the first move in Bassai Dai?).

Judo and sumo are also the same. In those arts, kicking is prohibited, and there are almost no jumping techniques. Practitioners need to stand firmly on the floor rather than jumping around; thus, the tucked-in pelvis gives more balance and stability to their stance.

On the other hand, in kung fu, especially in the Northern styles, there are a lot of kicks and jumps. From a low *kiba dachi*, I find it easier to jump and rotate the body quickly with the pelvis pushed back. Please try it and see if what I am saying makes sense.

Another thing I need to bring to your attention is the difference we see in the *zenkutsu dachi* between karate and kung fu. The first two photos below are from kung fu, and the last one (on the right) is of Yoshiharu Osaka (大坂 可治, 1947–), a JKA instructor. You can clearly see that the pelvis is pushed backward in the kung fu front stance, while Osaka Sensei definitely has his pelvis tucked in.

This, again, comes from the difference in the concept or the use of the stance. In other words, in kung fu, the moves are not always to the front but can be to the side, to the back, or in a rotation. As you can see in Osaka's very Shotokan-style technique, it is a strong *oi zuki* going straight forward. For this move, tucking the pelvis in, aligning the fist with the rear foot, and keeping the backbone straight produces the most powerful technique. The principle of the karate punch is *ikken hissatsu* (一拳必殺), meaning 'one punch, certain kill', while kung fu attacks are multiple, and each punch or attack may not be a "sure kill" technique.

As a bonus, I will share with you another interesting point. Take a look at the photos at the top of the next page.

The first two photos are from Okinawan Shorin Ryu (沖縄小林流). In the first photo, Master Choshin Chibana (知花朝信, 1885–1969), is doing Passai (our Bassai) and is keeping his pelvis somewhat tucked in, but the second photo shows that the pelvis is positioned more toward the back. Regardless of the pelvis position, you will notice that both of them are leaning forward, which is similar to the kung fu practitioners shown earlier. The practitioners in the third photo show a technique from Bassai Dai. They are from Shito Ryu and Shotokan, respectively.

You can assume that the original Okinawan karate kept some of the Chinese influence, but when karate was introduced into Japan, it changed with the influence of the Japanese martial arts. In the Japanese martial arts, such as kendo and even karate, we are taught to always keep our upper body straight and to never crouch forward or lean to the sides. I suspect that the influence on our posture in our karate came mainly from jujutsu and kendo. The posture of judo practitioners has changed drastically since judo became an Olympic sport in 1964, but that is a different subject that is not directly related to the topic at hand, so I will not discuss it here, though it is a very interesting subject to think about.

So, you can probably easily guess what my theory for Master Asai's posture is. You probably want to conclude that the kung fu influence he received in Taiwan changed his posture. However, maybe to your surprise, my theory is slightly different. Master Asai was known for his *tenshin* techniques, but, at the same time, he was known for his high and low techniques. A low technique is one in which he ducks. For example, he would dodge a kick by going underneath. A high technique is one in which he jumps around an opponent and hits him while he is still in the air (see photo below).

I do not believe he learned those techniques from White Crane kung fu or from any other style. The characteristic techniques of White Crane kung fu are open-hand techniques and whipping techniques (coming from rapid wing flapping). I can easily suspect that he took those techniques in and made them into his signature techniques. However, jumping and ducking, I believe, were his own creation.

Look at this famous photo (left) of him fighting Mikami Sensei (JKA Louisiana) in the JKA's All Japan Championship in 1961. Mikami (left) is delivering a beautiful long-distance *oi zuki*, very much a Shotokan technique. You can see that Asai (right) jumped to dodge this attack—I wish I could have been there to watch it. This shows that he was already jumping in his early karate career—he was twenty-six years old in 1961.

He was a very creative martial artist, and I understand that he always tried different things and new ideas that would work for him. Even for a Japanese, he was a small man (a little over 5'3" [160 cm] and less than 110 lbs. [50 kg]), so he needed techniques that would overcome his "handicap." He discovered jumping and *tenshin* techniques. In order to jump and rotate his body quickly, not tucking in his pelvis worked better for him. He probably developed his unique posture early in his karate career, but his peculiar pelvis position was not that noticeable then. With many years of training, which included kung fu techniques, his posture became more prominent and more noticeable.

Here are two photos (below) of Master Asai at two different stages of his karate life. The one on the left is a young Asai doing Nijushiho in his twenties, and the one on the right is of him doing a legendary deep stance in his sixties.

What do you think? It is true that he went to Taiwan and that he had a close encounter with White Crane kung fu, but there were, I assume, many other Shotokan practitioners who went to China and Taiwan. In fact, Mas-

ter Nakayama was stationed in China for several years during World War II.
Only Asai picked up many ideas and techniques from the Chinese styles. This
proves my point that his body was far more adaptable to the Chinese method
because of his own unique training and his own style.

I am not a hundred percent sure if my theory about his pelvis position is
correct, but one thing I can confidently say is this. Master Asai needed his pelvis positioned that way to deliver his fast and unique techniques. He was the
one and only true master of Asai Ryu karate, and his posture is a signature of
his style.

CHAPTER FOURTEEN
第十四章

THE IRONY OF FUNAKOSHI'S TEACHING METHOD
船越先生教授法の悲劇

First, I must start this chapter with this photo here. I have known about this photo for a long time. It is a famous photo showing Funakoshi with Chojun Miyagi (宮城長順, 1888–1953), the founder of Goju Ryu. Miyagi visited Tokyo in 1932, ten years after Funakoshi migrated to mainland Japan. In the back, you can see two of Funakoshi's students. The one on the left is Yasuhiro Konishi (小西康裕, 1893–1983), who founded Shindo Jinen Ryu (神道自然流). I was able to recognize Konishi but was ignorant about who the person standing between Funakoshi and Miyagi was. Some people later informed me that this person's name was Yamada and that he was the founder of Nihon Kenpo Karatedo (日本拳法空手道), a full-contact karate style. This is different from Nippon Kempo (日本拳法), also known as Nikken (日拳), a style that uses full armor similar to that which is used in kendo. Since I am not familiar with either of these, I will not venture into the differentiation between them in this chapter.

I did some research on Yamada, and here is a short story about this interesting man. His full name is Yamada Tatsuo (山田辰雄, 1905–1967). He was born in 1905 in a city in Hyogo Prefecture near my hometown, Kobe. He started his martial arts training in jujutsu when he was in elementary school then moved on to judo training at the Kodokan when he was seventeen. This was when he encountered karate. Funakoshi began to teach karate at the Kodokan that very year, 1922, just when Yamada took up judo training. Apparently, he also became a student of Funakoshi and started his karate training. I do not know if he continued his judo training.

Regardless, after only two years of training with Funakoshi, he moved to Osaka so that he could join the dojo of Choki Motobu, the founder of Motobu Ryu (本部流). Motobu was one of the few Okinawan masters who came to mainland Japan to teach *te* (手) in the early twentieth century. Unfortunately, he did not have a good reputation as he could not speak the Japanese language and his training was very rough. He did not teach too many *kata*, but his train-

ing consisted of a lot of *bunkai* and sparring. Yamada obviously was looking for the "real" fighting method, so he moved to Osaka to receive his teaching. He must have done well because Motobu published the book *Okinawa Kenpo Karate-jutsu Kumite-hen* (沖縄拳法唐手術組手編) in 1926, in which he used Yamada as his *kumite* partner (photo left). In general, however, Motobu's teaching was not that successful in Japan even though he stayed there (in Tokyo and then in Osaka)

for nearly twenty years. Due to World War II, most young people were drafted into the military in the thirties. After losing almost all his students, Motobu decided to return to Okinawa in 1941 and died there three years later.

Choki Motobu: http://en.wikipedia.org/wiki/Motobu_Ch%C5%8Dki

Yasuhiro Konishi: http://en.wikipedia.org/wiki/Yasuhiro_Konishi

Hironori Otsuka: http://en.wikipedia.org/wiki/Hironori_%C5%8Ctsuka

Kenwa Mabuni: http://en.wikipedia.org/wiki/Kenwa_Mabuni

Here is another famous photo of the karate masters gathered after a martial arts festival by the Dai Nippon Butokukai (大日本武徳会) in 1938. In the front row, far left, is Tatsuo Yamada. You can see Otsuka, Mabuni, Yamaguchi, Konishi, and many other no-

tables. It is curious that Funakoshi and Motobu are not in the photo.

After the war, Yamada finally opened his own dojo in Tokyo (1955) and called it Nihon Kenpo Karatedo. In fact, this resulted in a new karate style. He was the first karate practitioner to come up with the idea of using protective gear for full-contact karate training. He later introduced a full-contact tournament without any protective gear except for a pair of gloves.

In the fifties, Mas Oyama was trying to gain recognition but was not successful initially because he was Korean and also because he promoted a full-contact karate style, Kyokushinkai karate. Yamada and Oyama got acquainted and exchanged students for cross-training. To promote full-contact karate, Oyama went overseas and challenged professional wrestlers to knockout matches. Here is a photo of a welcome-home party for Oyama in the late fifties (left). You can see that Yamada was one of the guests (back row, third from the right).

On the other hand, Yamada made an announcement in November 1959 that he had a plan called *The Draft Principles of Project of Establishment of a New Sport and Its Industrialization*. In other words, he came up with new *kumite* rules, which allowed full contact using gloves, and called this *karateboxing*, but, unfortunately, it did not catch on as it was so new. At that time, it was unimaginable to hit each other in karate matches in Japan.

He was also impressed with Thai kickboxing; thus, he contributed a lot when the Kickboxing Association was founded in 1966. On December 20, 1959, the very first Muay Thai tournament was held in Tokyo. It is still unknown whether Thai fighters were invited by Yamada, but it is clear that Yamada was the only *karateka* at that time who was really interested in Muay Thai. Later on, Mas Oyama also showed an interest in Muay Thai and sent his students to the Muay Thai matches.

Yamada invited a Muay Thai champion from Thailand and started studying Muay Thai. At that time, Osamu Noguchi (野口修, 1934–), a boxing promoter, showed interest in Muay Thai. Tatsuo Yamada and Osamu Noguchi met and worked together to create Muay Thai vs. karate matches, in which opponents could hit and kick each other. It was actually Osamu Noguchi who coined the term *kickboxing*, and, after several matches, this new martial art gained popularity and spread fairly quickly.

Yamada hosted a special event called *Karate vs. Muay Thai Fights*, held on February 12, 1963. Around that time, Mas Oyama became interested in Muay Thai matches and sent three of his Kyokushin *karateka* to the Lumpinee Boxing Stadium in Thailand. They fought against three Muay Thai fighters. The three Kyokushin karate fighters' names were Tadashi Nakamura, Kenji Kurosaki, and Akio Fujihira (also known as Noboru Osawa). Nakamura and Fujihira won, while Kurosaki lost.

Noguchi studied Muay Thai and developed a combined martial art, which he named *kickboxing*. This art absorbed and adopted more rules than techniques from Muay Thai. The main techniques of kickboxing are still derived from Japanese full-contact karate, Kyokushinkai. However, throwing and headbutting were allowed in the beginning to distinguish it from Muay Thai. This was later repealed, and these techniques were banned. The Kickboxing Association was founded by Osamu Noguchi in 1966.

Kickboxing not only became very popular but also evolved into the K-2 and MMA of today. The rightful credit should be given to its founders, Yamada and Noguchi. Unfortunately, Yamada suffered from liver cancer and died in 1967 at the young age of sixty-two.

Interestingly, Yamada's first name was *Tatsuo*(辰雄), which means 'Dragon Man'. As his name dictates, he spent his entire life in pursuit of a martial art with fierce fighting. Unfortunately, he could not win the battle against cancer.

Masutatsu Oyama: http://en.wikipedia.org/wiki/Mas_Oyama
Kyokushin karate: http://en.wikipedia.org/wiki/Kyokushin
Kickboxing: http://en.wikipedia.org/wiki/Kickboxing

The main purpose of this chapter is not to introduce Yamada but to present a very ironic development of karate from Funakoshi's teachings. I can almost call it a tragedy or perhaps black humor. Let me explain. It is a well-known fact that Funakoshi's training syllabus was mostly *kata*. I am sure he also explained some *bunkai*, but, as you can imagine, he must have kept *bunkai* only for a few advanced students. For most of the beginning and intermediate students, he provided *kata* training only. This practice led to dissatisfaction on the part of many of the younger university students who demanded *kumite*, or sparring-type training.

Let me give you some examples of dissatisfied students as many of them became well known. Konishi, who was pictured standing on the far left in the very first photo of this chapter, was one of them. He was an experienced *kendoka* before he joined Funakoshi's dojo. Konishi openly sought out the teaching of other masters, including Motobu and Mabuni, the founder of Shito Ryu. He founded his own style, Shindo Jinen Ryu, after he departed from Funakoshi. Another unhappy student was Hironori Otsuka (大塚博紀, 1892–1982 [photo left]), who was an experienced *jujutsuka* who would later be the founder of Wado Ryu (和道流).

With the training experience in kendo and jujutsu of these two students

(Konishi and Otsuka), they introduced the idea of *kihon kumite* to Funako-shi. Though Funakoshi was not totally happy with this idea, he almost had to adopt it to satisfy the strong demands of the young university students who complained about the lack of *kumite*-type training. Just as Yamada had done, both Konishi and Otsuka would eventually depart from Funakoshi. All three of them created their own styles (without Funakoshi's blessing, of course).

There was another episode. Tokyo University Karate Club was one of the universities in Tokyo that were following Funakoshi's teachings. In 1929, Fu-nakoshi discovered, by chance, that the karate club students at this university were secretly practicing free sparring, *jiyu kumite*. He got so upset that he resigned from his teaching position. A few years later, Otsuka began to teach at Tokyo University Karate Club, and the style was changed to Wado Ryu.

In addition, it is not very well known, but Mas Oyama joined Shotokan in the late forties and trained under Funakoshi for two years. He was also not satisfied with *kata*-only training, so he left and joined Goju Ryu. Eventually, he started his own style, Kyokushinkai, when he opened his own dojo in 1953.

I am sure this development did not make Funakoshi happy. I can easily imagine that this troubled him a lot. I can only guess that he could not under-stand why so many of his talented students would leave him and start other karate styles that were unlike what he had been teaching. He was a teacher throughout his career, so he must have been confident that he was a good teacher. He also believed in the martial arts and in what he was teaching. This is why he did not allow any *jiyu kumite* or permit *shiai* ('tournaments') all the way up to his death.

The final bit of trivia in this chapter is what hap-pened between Funakoshi and the Nihon Karate Kyokai (日本空手協会 [JKA]). When the JKA was es-tablished in 1948, Funakoshi accepted the position of Chief Instructor. However, a very strange thing happened after a few years. Funakoshi resigned this

position in the early fifties (formally in 1956), but this news was not publicly announced. The reason for this has been hidden and has become almost taboo to JKA practitioners even now.

Some have claimed that Funakoshi was sandwiched between the JKA and the Shotokai (松濤會), Egami's group. According to these people, Funakoshi supposedly did not want to show any favoritism to one organization. But, this is an illogical explanation as Funakoshi kept his chairman position at the Shotokai until his death in 1957. Others have said that Funakoshi was getting too old to hold the position—he was eighty-four in 1952. But, in fact, the position he had was an honorary one, and he really did not need to do anything except show up at the *shihankai* (師範会, 'board of directors meetings') if he wanted to. His health was pretty good until his passing at the age of eighty-eight, so his age might not have been the only reason.

I am the first one to publicly share the true reason, but, before I jump in to the reason, I need to ask the reader to understand what Japan was like in the late forties and early fifties. This information is very important and has a lot of impact on how Shotokan karate developed in the second half of the twentieth century.

Japan lost World War II in 1945. She was occupied by the Allied forces (called *GHQ*, which consisted mainly of the U.S. Army under the command of General Douglas MacArthur) between 1945 and 1952. For a few years, all martial arts were totally banned. Senior karate instructors such as Nakayama and Obata worked very hard to get permission from GHQ to organize and practice karate publicly. The story about this effort itself deserves a full chapter, but we will not go into it in this chapter.

As you can see, the JKA was established in 1948, and it turned out that karate was the first art to receive such permission. For instance, kendo was tied to the samurai and thus considered a source of aggression. It had to wait till 1950 to get permission to form an organization and practice publicly. Regardless, toward the end of the war, Japan was devastated as it had literally been flattened by the carpet bombing of U.S. bombers (B-29s) as well as two atomic bombs. Needless to say, everyone was extremely poor, and, in fact, some citizens died of starvation.

The JKA could not pay any of its instructors, so all instructors had to maintain side jobs to stay alive. The JKA opened its doors to the public to practice karate, but few showed up as the general public was too poor to afford a membership fee. Besides, they had to work long hours just to live and did not have free time to practice karate. So, Nakayama had to be very creative to attract newcomers and to keep students.

During the occupation period, GHQ brought American culture to Japan. It was called the *Three-S Culture*, which stood for *sports*, *sex*, and *screen* (i.e., Hollywood movies). They were to give the Japanese people entertainment as well as a nonaggressive mentality. The game of baseball became a national sport in Japan almost instantaneously and is still the most popular sport even to this date. TVs were also brought in the fifties, so sumo matches and professional wrestling also became very popular. Many people would gather around TV sets at electronics shops or bathhouses, which I remember clearly though I was only around ten years old.

Soon Nakayama realized that a big tournament would attract a lot of people. He consulted with Funakoshi about organizing a national championship in

Tokyo and found that Funakoshi was totally against this idea. The Shotokai group promised him that they would not hold any tournaments, so Funakoshi began to spend more time with the Shotokai. As a result, he decreased his presence with the JKA in the last few years of his life. Funakoshi passed in April of 1957, and the JKA held its first national championship six

months later. This was not by accident. Nakayama showed his respect by not having held a tournament while Funakoshi was still alive.

What is ironic is that, thanks to Nakayama's great leadership and his creative idea, which Funakoshi opposed, the JKA became very successful, and its organizational size grew much larger than that of the Shotokai. The JKA was the first and most aggressive organization to dispatch many young and talented instructors around the world in the sixties, which contributed to the achievement of Shotokan and its being the most popular karate style in the world. *Shiai* and sport karate are becoming more and more popular. Some people are trying very hard to get karate added as an event in the 2020 Tokyo Olympics.

Funakoshi really wanted to keep the martial art part in karate, so I wonder if he would approve of the current trend. I believe it is now time for all of us to think deeply about what the true meaning of *success* is in Shotokan karate. It is not too late for us to bring Shotokan karate back to being a martial art and teach our students to practice and live by both the *Dojo Kun* and the *Niju Kun*. In the epilogue, I will state my interpretation of each *kun* and try to explain what Funakoshi wanted to teach us through the *Niju Kun*.

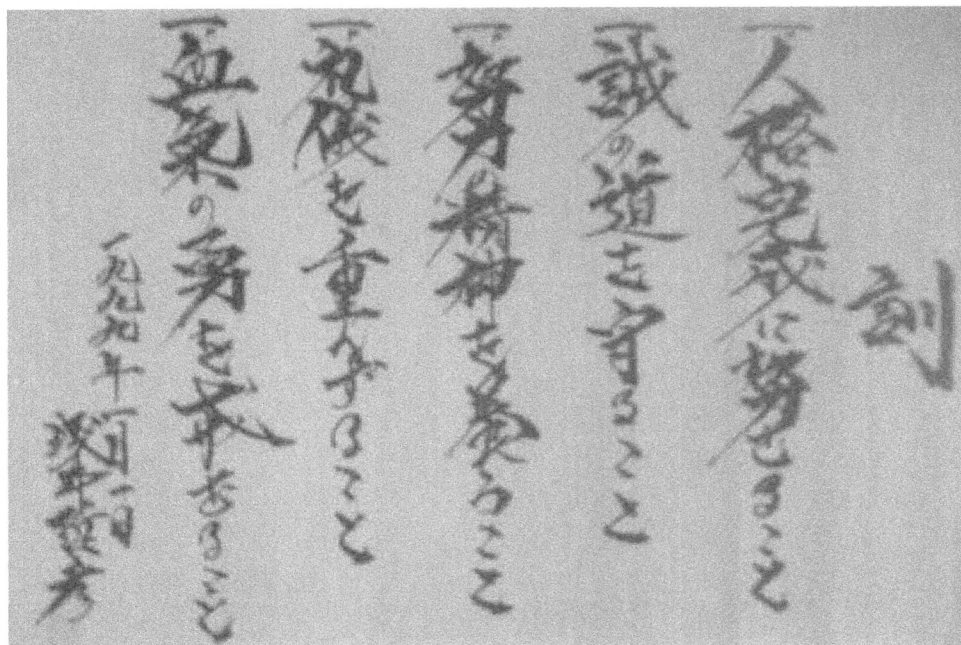

Dojo Kun written by Master Asai

EPILOGUE

エピローグ

FUNAKOSHI NIJU KUN
TWENTY TEACHINGS OF
MASTER FUNAKOSHI

空手二十箇條

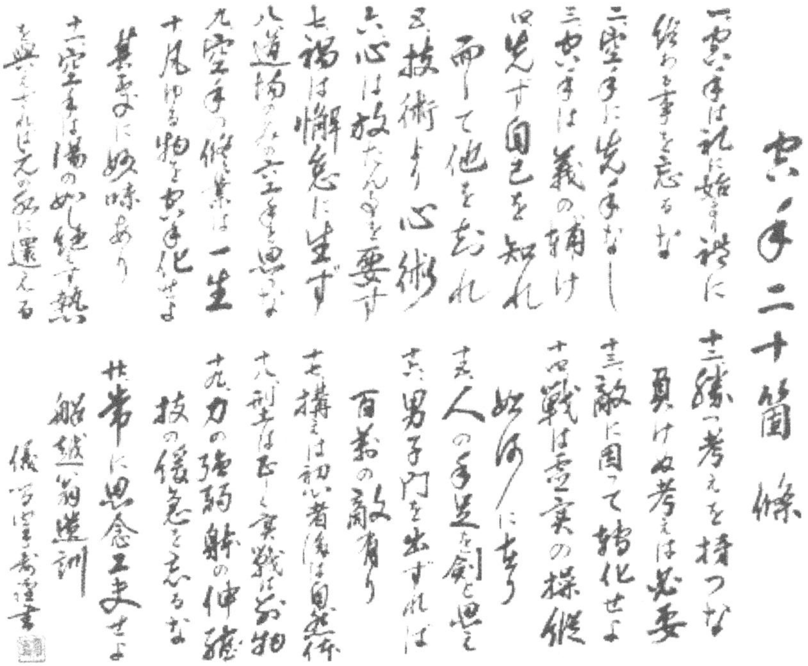

空手二十箇條

一、空手は礼に始まり礼に終る事を忘るな

二、空手に先手なし

三、空手は義の補け

四、先づ自己を知れ而して他を知れ

五、技術より心術

六、心は放たんことを要す

七、禍は懈怠に生ず

八、道場のみの空手と思ふな

九、空手の修業は一生である

十、凡ゆるものを空手化せよ其處に妙味あり

十一、空手は湯の如し絶えず熱を與えざれば元の水に還える

十二、勝つ考えは持つな負けぬ考えは必要

十三、敵に因って轉化せよ

十四、戰は虚實の操縦如何に在り

十五、人の手足を劍と思え

十六、男子門を出ずれば百萬の敵あり

十七、構えは初心者に後は自然體

十八、型は正しく實戰は別物

十九、力の強弱體の伸縮技の緩急を忘るな

二十、常に思念工夫せよ

船越義珍遺訓

儀書

Gichin Funakoshi created both the *Dojo Kun*, in which five principles are found, and the *Niju Kun*, in which twenty more principles are described. I suspect that Funakoshi wanted to make the *Dojo Kun* to cover only a few precepts so that the students could recite it daily. He ended up with the five most important ones. However, there were many more teachings he wanted to hand down, so these became the second *kun*, which was originally named *Karate Niju Kajo* (空手二十箇條, '*Karate Twenty Principles*'). Now it is commonly called *Shotokan Niju Kun* (松濤館二十訓) or simply *Niju Kun* (二十訓).

Niju means 'twenty', and *kun* literally means 'motto' or 'teaching'. The *Niju Kun* is a valuable list of twenty mottoes we can use to seek the way of karate. But, in the end, you must apply these twenty mottoes to your life through the practice of karate. The *Niju Kun* has a *Wikipedia* page, and each *kun* is translated there: http://en.wikipedia.org/wiki/Nij%C5%AB_kun.

I will refer to the translation by *Wikipedia* as it is the most popularly accepted. I must say that the translation of some of the *kun* found on *Wikipedia* is good, but I find most of them needing corrections and further explanation. I will include additional information here to complete the meaning of each *kun*.

Just as shown in *Wikipedia*, I will list each *kun* in Japanese then in *romaji* (ローマ字, 'roman letters') followed up by the *Wikipedia* translation. Then, I will put my explanation at the end.

1. 空手道は礼に始まり礼に終る事を忘るな
Karatedo wa rei ni hajimari rei ni owaru koto o wasuru na
Karatedo begins and ends with bowing.

It is true that the word *rei* (礼) can be translated as 'bow'. So, it is true that we always start our *kata* with a bow and end it with another. However, here I believe Funakoshi was trying to say something that is deeper and more comprehensive. I believe he wanted to cover general etiquette and respect with this *kun*. You can find another word in the fourth principle of the *Dojo Kun*, *reigi* (礼儀), which means 'good manners'. So, the meaning of this *kun* should be understood as we must not forget that *karatedo* means to always live with good manners, whether you are inside or outside the dojo.

2. 空手に先手なし

Karate ni sente nashi

There is no first strike in karate.

This is commonly translated as 'there is no first strike in karate', but the meaning of this *kun* is deeper. He did not literally mean that we must not throw the first strike. He meant that we must not instigate or cause a fight. But, once it becomes obvious or clear that we must defend ourselves, we must do what is absolutely necessary, including striking first. On Okinawa, there is another popular saying, *sente hissho*, which means 'a first attack always brings a victory'.

3. 空手は義の補け

Karate wa gi no tasuke

Karate stands on the side of justice.

Wikipedia's translation, unfortunately, makes the meaning of this one unclear. *Gi* (義) means 'righteousness' or 'justice'. *Tasuke* (補け) means 'to supplement' or 'to supply'. So, this means that, by practicing karate, we must always abide by the laws and do what is right.

4. 先づ自己を知れ而して他を知れ

Mazu onore o shire shikashite ta o shire

First know yourself, then know others.

Funakoshi was an educated person, so he knew about Sun Tzu and his famous book, *The Art of War*. In it, Sun Tzu said, "If you know the enemy and know yourself, you need not fear the result of a hundred battles." There are two interesting points here. One is that Funakoshi said, "*First* know yourself," while Sun Tzu listed the enemy first. I think this is extremely important as it comes from Bushido philosophy. Another interesting point is that Funakoshi said to know others instead of the enemy. I think Funakoshi's teaching was more comprehensive and that you can apply it to your daily life both in peace and in war or battle. I am not saying Sun Tzu's teaching is less valuable. I am simply stating that his idea focused only on war.

5. 技術より心術

Gijutsu yori shinjutsu

Mentality over technique.

This translation needs further explanation to understand the deep meaning of this *kun*. Let me explain the meaning of each word, and that should help us understand this important *kun*. *Gijutsu* (技術) means 'technique', but *gi* (技) itself means 'technique', and *jutsu* (術) means 'art', 'way', 'method', or 'means'. So, it means 'technical method' or 'technical way'. So, it does not necessarily mean 'karate techniques'. When we say the word *gijutsusha* (技術者), that is, '*gijutsu* person', we mean 'engineer' or 'craftsman'. Regardless, by "*gijutsu*," he was referring to karate techniques.

Then, what is *shinjutsu* (心術)? *Shin* (心) means 'heart', 'mind', or 'intelligence'. So, we may quickly translate *shinjutsu* as 'mind way' or 'intelligent way'; however, this translation is not exactly what Funakoshi really wanted to say.

The Japanese word *shin* has many meanings, and it is a very important word in Japanese. *Shin* can mean 'center' or 'core' (*kan* [幹]) and even 'stomach' or 'guts' (*hara* [腹]). The samurai considered *shin* and *hara* to be the center of their samurai spirit or value. This is why they cut their belly open when they committed *seppuku* (切腹), or *harakiri* (腹切), to show that their center was pure.

I do not think Funakoshi was thinking of *harakiri*, but he was thinking of the samurai spirit. He was thinking of the *gojo no toku* (五常の徳), which are the five cardinal Confucian virtues. These virtues are *jin* (仁, 'benevolence'), *gi* (義, 'justice'), *rei* (礼, 'courtesy'), *chi* (智, 'wisdom'), and *shin* (信, 'trust'). I will write about Bushido in the near future and will include further explanation of the *gojo no toku* at that time.

In short, Funakoshi put the essence in the *Dojo Kun* he created. He did not deny the need for karate training but wanted to emphasize the importance of the mental and spiritual or ethical part of self-development. He put the concept in a very short sentence, and I suspect that he spent a lot of time with the students, explaining what he really meant by this *kun*.

6. 心は放たん事を要す
Kokoro wa hanatan koto o yosu
The heart must be set free.

This is another difficult one. Interestingly, the same kanji is used here, i.e., 心. The direct translation of 'the heart must be set free' does not make sense to most readers. As you can see, the pronunciation of the kanji is different in this *kun* as here it is read *kokoro*. Even though the literal translation of *kokoro* is 'heart', Funakoshi meant something deeper. It is closer, I should say, to the psychological sense and could be translated as 'mind'. In other words, he was stating that we tend to get trapped in one way and do not see other options or methods. To practice and improve in karate, we must not be trapped in one way or one method. One good example may be *bunkai*. You may believe one *bunkai* is correct, but you need to open your mind and consider other options. He wanted us to be flexible with our mind and our thinking.

7. 禍は懈怠に生ず

Wazawai wa ketai ni seizu

Calamity springs from carelessness.

The translation I find here is unfortunately incorrect. The first kanji, *wazawai* (禍), is not really 'calamity' in this context. He meant rather a smaller problem or an accident. The next word, *ketai* (懈怠) is a difficult one, and it means 'to be lazy' or 'to slack off'. He wanted to warn us that if we slack off in our training or whatever else in our life, it may result in an accident or a problem. He is telling us to be a hundred percent concentrated on and dedicated to karate training.

8. 道場のみの空手と思うな

Dojo nomi no karate to omou na

Karate goes beyond the dojo.

The translation here can be expanded a little, though most readers understand what this *kun* means. Some may misunderstand that the meaning of this *kun* is limited only to self-defense and danger outside of the dojo. Of course, that is included here, but this *kun* covers much more. He wanted to tell us that all the virtues (mentioned above) and self-discipline must be applied to our daily life. He also expected us to pay much attention to the true concept of self-defense, which involves almost every action in your daily life (be sure to thoroughly read Chapter 9: "What Is 'Complete' Self-Defense?" on this specific subject). His expectation was really high, but he could do this as he exemplified it with his own actions. He rarely got sick in his adult life and lived to be eighty-nine years old.

9. 空手の修業は一生である

Karatedo no shugyo wa isssho de aru

Karate is a lifelong pursuit.

The translation in *Wikipedia* is not wrong, but the word *shugyo* (修業) needs to be explained to better understand the meaning of this *kun*. It means 'study', 'learn', or 'train'. Therefore, I prefer to translate this *kun* as 'karate training is a lifelong pursuit'. This was the reason why Master Asai did not accept a tenth *dan* during his lifetime. He said he was still pursuing perfect karate, which he said he had not found. I believe Master Asai kept this *kun* and lived by it.

10. 凡ゆるものを空手化せよ其処に妙味あり

Arayuru mono o karate kaseyo soko ni myomi ari

Apply the way of karate to all things. Therein lies its beauty.

I agree with the translation, but the second one needs further explanation. The word *myomi* (妙味) is a difficult one to translate. It literally means 'good taste', 'charm' or 'profit'. If you can expand the benefits of karate to your life, you can really enjoy your life.

For an example, Master Funakoshi was always healthy until his death at eighty-nine years old. He said he was applying self-defense against illness. Another example is avoiding accidents (in an automobile or just falling down), and there are many others. So, the translation is 'beauty', but it really means 'true benefit' or 'enjoyment [in life]'.

11. 空手は湯の如し絶えず熱を与えざれば元の水に還る

Karate wa yu no gotoshi taezu netsu o ataeza-reba moto no mizu ni kaeru

Karate is like boiling water; without heat, it returns to its tepid state.

I agree with this translation, and there is no need of further explanation.

12. 勝つ考えは持つな負けぬ考えは必要

Katsu kangae wa motsu na makenu kangae wa hitsuyo

Do not think of winning. Think, rather, of not losing.

The translation is fine. In the case competitors, you may wonder whether you should fight to a draw if you are not supposed to be thinking of winning or losing. Of course, Master Funakoshi was surely not thinking this as he opposed any tournament or competition. So, I assume he was talking about a real fight. With this somewhat contradictory *kun*, he was telling us that the ultimate aim is to not get into any fight or conflict.

13. 敵に因って轉化せよ

Teki ni yotte tenka seyo

Make adjustments according to your opponent.

I want to mention that *teki* (敵) is more than just an opponent. It refers to an enemy or a challenge in general. Therefore, he was not talking about adjusting only to the people you fight but also to all possible challenges you may face in your life, including natural disasters, accidents, and illness.

14. 戦は虚実の操縦如何に在り

Tatakai wa kyojitsu no soju ikan ni ari

The outcome of a battle depends on how one handles emptiness and fullness (weakness and strength).

This *kun* is a challenging one to translate, and what makes it difficult is the kanji for the word *kyojitsu* (虚実). Let's investigate the meaning of these two characters. *Kyo* (虚) literally means 'imaginary', 'hollow', 'falsehood' or 'fake'. On the other hand, *jitsu* (実) means the opposite, including 'truth', 'reality', and 'substance'.

Then, another word, *soju* (操縦), is translated as 'handles', which is not incorrect, but the word *handle* has a passive sense to it. In fact, *soju* is more aggressive, meaning 'control' or 'drive'. So, this could be translated as 'the outcome of a battle depends on how one controls falsehood and reality'.

In a *kumite* situation, it could be a fake technique and a real technique. However, the first kanji, *tatakai* (戦), does not necessarily refer to a battle against an enemy. Funakoshi was thinking larger. He was referring to all the battles in your life, such as sickness, finances, work, etc.

When he migrated to Japan, he was already fifty-four years old. He was a respected school teacher on Okinawa, but when he moved to Tokyo, he had no place to live. For many years, he had to live in the school's very small maintenance room. He used to say with a smile on his face that he had a small bedroom but the backyard was huge. Of course, it was not a backyard but the school campus. He won the battle against poverty by controlling his mind.

15. 人の手足を剣と思え

Hito no teashi o ken to omoe

Think of hands and feet as swords.

This is a simple one, and the translation is fine. I would just like to add that Funakoshi truly believed in this concept. You can see this in at least two things he did.

One is that he chose not to include Sanchin *kata* or its training method, which is a very popular *kata* among the Naha Te styles, such as Goju Ryu and Uechi Ryu. I have written in one of my books that Funakoshi created the new stance *hangetsu dachi* from *sanchin dachi*. What he rejected was not the *kata* itself but its training method, in which a sensei would hit and kick the performer to check his *chinkuchi* (チンクチ, 'body tension'). This is an exercise to prepare the practitioner for getting punched and kicked. Funakoshi thought such an exercise or preparation was useless as he believed that the opponent's hands and feet were swords. His concept was to not get hit at all.

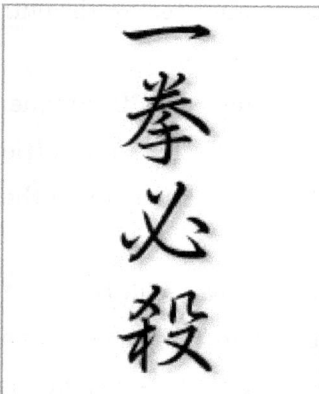

The other action by Funakoshi was the rejection of the tournament concept. He had a few reasons to oppose this. One of them was his belief that a karate technique must be improved to the point of *ikken hissatsu*, which means 'one punch, certain kill'. Just as you do not have a tournament with real swords, he considered it impossible to have a tournament using karate techniques at full speed and power.

Despite strong opposition by Funakoshi, the JKA went ahead with the first All Japan Championship in 1957. It has been more than fifty years since the introduction of large-scale tournaments into Japan. Considering that Funakoshi believed that the hands and feet were swords, it is rather ironic that no one has been killed or even seriously injured in any of the major tournaments in Japan so far. This would be another interesting subject to discuss further at another opportunity.

16. 男子門を出づれば百万の敵あり
Danshi mon o izureba hyakuman no teki ari
When you step beyond your own gate, you face a million enemies.

This is a literal translation of the Japanese *kun*. *Hyakuman* (百万) means 'one million', but it also means simply 'a lot'. This is the same usage as in the English phrase "thanks a million." So, I think '...you face many enemies' is a more appropriate translation.

17. 構は初心者に後は自然体
Kamae wa shoshinsha ni ato wa shizentai
Formal stances are for beginners; later, one stands naturally.

This translation is, unfortunately, a poor one. The words *formal stances* are not clear or accurate. We know what *kamae* (構) means; it is a fighting stance. We also know the word *shizentai* (自然体), and it was translated correctly. It is a natural stance. The tricky part is the translation of the words *ato wa* (後は). The literal meaning is 'later', but the question is how much later. It is not a few minutes or even a day later. The time span is much longer as it refers to when a beginner gets to be an advanced practitioner. So, a better translation may be 'a fighting stance is only for beginners; when they become advanced, they should fight from a natural stance'.

18. 形は正しく実戦は別物

Kata wa tadashiku, jissen wa betsumono

Perform prescribed sets of techniques exactly; actual combat is another matter.

I can tell that the translator had a big challenge with this *kun*. The translator intentionally changed the meaning of *kata* (形). I do not know why as we all know that *kata* is *kata*, though 'prescribed sets of techniques' is not totally wrong. However, the translation is done for karate practitioners and not for the general public. Thus, this word should be kept as *kata*. Funakoshi stated that we should do the *kata* correctly, which means he did not want us to change or modify them. The translation for the second part is acceptable. I prefer 'actual fighting is a different story'.

He wrote this *kun* as, I suspect, many university students wanted to change the *kata*. There was also a big difference between the performance of the *kata* and the movements in the *bunkai*. He must have spent a lot of energy explaining the reasons for the difference; however, I am afraid the students did not possess the necessary skills to understand what Funakoshi meant. He wanted to impress upon them that the *kata* must be done as they were taught.

This brings up a very interesting point as Funakoshi was the one who changed and modified the *kata* he brought from Okinawa. I know he received a lot of criticism from the masters on Okinawa at that time, but he believed those changes were needed. I agree with most of them, though, with great respect, I disagree with the rest. One good example of my disagreement is

that he switched all *neko ashi dachi* to *kokutsu dachi*. Another is his change of *sanchin dachi* to *hangetsu dachi*. In other words, he de-emphasized short stances and focused on long and low stances. I suspect that his son Gigo had a big influence on this. I should write about this one day.

19. 力の強弱体の伸縮技の緩急を忘るな

Chikara no kyojaku tai no shinshuku waza no kankyu o wasuruna

Do not forget the employment or withdrawal of power, the extension or contraction of the body, the swift or leisurely application of technique.

This is another challenging *kun*, and it contains three essential elements of karate. I consider this *kun* to be one of the most important from the perspective of karate training. Let's look at these three elements.

The first one is *chikara no kyojaku* (力の強弱). *Chikara* (力) is the power that a practitioner executes. *Kyojaku* (強弱) literally means 'strong and weak'. So, Funakoshi is saying you need to know when to use power and when not to. You see this in many of the advanced *kata*, and this must be the same in *kumite*. The teaching here is not to tense up all the time. Probably the most difficult thing is mastering how to change the level of power used. For instance, in *mawashi uke*, you need to start without tension (weak) and end with tension (strong). Another situation may be going from a strong *kime* technique to a following move that is slow and without tension (e.g., going from *oi zuki* [with *kiai*] to *heisoku dachi morote koshi kamae* in Heian Sandan).

The second one is *tai no shinshuku* (体の伸縮). *Tai* (体) means 'body', and *shinshuku* (伸縮) means 'expansion and contraction'. My sensei used to tell us to make our techniques big. I had some difficulty understanding him at that time, but now I understand that he wanted us to expand our body (as we were too tense). We need to extend our arms and legs when we execute many of the long techniques, such as *oi zuki*, *gyaku zuki*, *mae geri*, and *yoko geri*. Even for the straight blocking techniques, despite the blocking arm's being bent, you must expand the chest or back. Students tend to contract too much and fail to expand sufficiently.

The last one is *waza no kankyu* (技の緩急). *Waza* means 'techniques', and *kankyu* means 'fast and slow'. What is important is that this "fast and slow" is describing not only speed but also timing. I am afraid that Funakoshi would be crying if he could see how the *kata* have been modified in the tournaments. Not only the techniques themselves but also the speed and timing have been altered these days. I particularly see the *kata* done with extremely long pauses and also without the slow tempo or timing that is necessary. We must remember that the *kata* were created from actual fighting experience, and there is a well-thought-out reason behind each combination and sequence.

20. 常に思念工夫せよ

Tsune ni shinen kufu seyo

Be constantly mindful, diligent, and resourceful in your pursuit of the Way.

The literal translation of this *kun* is 'always think deeply (*shinen* [思念]) and be creative (*kufu* [工夫])'. The *Wikipedia* translation is much longer than what the Japanese *kun* says. The translator was correct by adding "in your pursuit of the Way" as this *kun* is not only for karate training but also for the pursuit of the Way (*do* [道]), *karatedo*.

I suspect that Funakoshi purposely placed this *kun* at the very end. He was blamed by many Okinawan masters for having made many changes not only to the karate techniques, such as the stances, but also to many of the cultural aspects that went along with karate, including the names of the *kata*, the uniform (*gi*), the *dan* ranks, etc. I am sure he hesitated in making those changes, but, after deep consideration, he made those changes because he believed they were necessary. This was not simply to justify his behavior; rather, he felt that this stance or attitude was absolutely necessary if you were to pursue the way of *karatedo* in your life. He was telling us how to get to the *ha* (破) stage of *shuhari* (守破離). He, of course, meant this to apply to more than just practicing karate. He wanted us to follow this path and apply it to everything in our lives. Let us continue our exciting karate journey and search for the Way (道).

道